Teriyaki Priest

Teriyaki Priest
Tales From the Realm of Gratitude

J.K. Hirano

BUDDHIST EDUCATION CENTER

Teriyaki Priest:
Tales From the Realm of Gratitude

Copyright 2013, J.K. Hirano
Published by Buddhist Education Center
Anaheim, California

Cover design, photography and illustration
by Stace Hasegawa

ISBN 978-0-9721395-8-8
Printed in the USA

This book is dedicated to the late
Rev. Russell Hamada, who opened the doors for
me to appreciate the realm of gratitude and whose
smile, laughter and friendship from the Pure Land
inspire me on a daily basis.

Many things occur in our human lives. But, whatever difficulties or sadness that we may have experienced, if we can look upon our lives as being rare and wondrous events, then we truly will have lived. If we are able to realize this realm of gratitude, in which we are able to live—and die—in gassho, then what else could we need?

Jitsuen Kakehashi,
Bearer of the Light: The Life and Thought of Rennyo

Table of Contents

Introduction

◆ ◆ ◆

At the encouragement of two of my best friends, my wife, Dr. Carmela Javellana Hirano, and my colleague, Rev. Marvin Harada, I am publishing this collection of essays I have written over the past 25 years as a Jodo Shinshu Buddhist minister. I guess 25 years of anything can be considered a long time by a young man; to an old man like me, the years have seemed to fly by. Living in the Dharma has made my life filled with gratitude for all the friends, family, and good and also difficult situations I have experienced. Obviously, being born and raised in Salt Lake City, Utah, becoming a Buddhist priest wasn't high on my list of occupational choices; but it was the best choice I could have possibly made.

When I was a child, Buddhism was something exotic, especially here in Salt Lake City, the headquarters of the Church of Jesus Christ of Latter Day Saints (LDS), the Mormons. Last year, 2012, our temple celebrated 100 years of Buddhism in Utah. It's amazing that Buddhism has been in Utah this long.

However, for many years, Buddhism was really only known in the Japanese American community. Our temple was not only the spiritual center of the community, but in many ways it was also the cultural center as well. The Judo Club was at the temple; the Japanese language school was also here. We were located in the center of Japantown. Kids going to our temple had weekday neighborhood friends and weekend temple friends. My weekday friends knew I was Buddhist, but they really didn't know what being Buddhist was. They just figured I was lucky not to have to go to their church all day Sunday or in the summer like them. My temple friends were third generation Japanese Americans like me, who also had two sets of friends. We temple friends had a very similar home life and religious background. We could also share certain secret codes like "5-4-4" (*goshishi* in Japanese). *Shishi* means "to urinate." We thought it was cool to be able to say "5-4-4" and know what it meant.

We knew that we were Buddhist, but it wasn't something you bragged about. The first time my weekday friends heard of anything Buddhist was when the television show *Kung Fu* came on. Kwai Chang Caine was a Shaolin Buddhist monk, wandering the Old West. When I became older and more politically conscious, I realized it wasn't right for a Caucasian man to play such a role, especially when it should have gone to Bruce Lee. Back in junior high and high school, when the show came on, the fact that here was an Asian Buddhist male who could really kick butt made me proud to be an Asian Buddhist male.

Since that time, Buddhism has become part of the American scene. The Dalai Lama is a spiritual superstar. Thich Nhat Hanh is a best selling author. Articles and books on meditation or Zen are commonly accessible and are read by many Americans. However, if you are still just an average American Jodo Shinshu Buddhist who doesn't have a shaved head or foreign accent, there are many who don't believe you can be a real Buddhist.

To kind of balance the scale of spiritual ignorance, there are even some Japanese who don't think Americans can really understand Jodo Shinshu. As a Jodo Shinshu Buddhist priest, having been born in Salt Lake City, Utah, and raised in a typical Japanese American family, I have to clearly state that Jodo Shinshu Buddhism is a clear Buddhist teaching for everyday life, and the beauty of our tradition is that you don't have to be a monk or know a foreign language to understand it.

I have taken these essays from the monthly articles I have written over the years for the temple newsletters from the San Jose Buddhist Church Betsuin, where I served from 1987-1993, and the Salt Lake Buddhist Temple, where I served from 1993 to the present. If you learn something about yourself in reading one of these essays, I will feel that it will all be worthwhile. But even if you don't, I have had a great 25 years trying to live and teach the Dharma.

Dharma isn't just about writing or reading it; it is about living, tasting, loving, laughing and crying with other human beings and realizing how grateful we should be, for we can't do it alone. The Buddha was once asked, "How important is the Sangha (fellowship of Buddhists) in understanding the Dharma?" He replied, "It is everything!" Thank you all for giving me everything in my life.

In Buddhism, the first Noble Truth is the statement "Life is suffering." This little statement has resulted in a lot of confusion about Buddhism by non-Buddhists. The suffering the Buddha referred to is the existential suffering of being human. The Buddha often listed four types of suffering: birth, old age, sickness and death. I have decided to sort these articles by these four types of suffering. I hope my writing will convey that Buddhism is a religion explaining what it means to be a human being.

The title "Teriyaki Priest" is in reference to the millions of chickens that have been eaten over the years to support our Buddhist Churches of America (BCA). It is in gratitude to all these chickens and people who have cooked and eaten them that I have been able to live my life as a priest. It is with deep gratitude that I bow to each of you, chickens and humans alike, who have allowed me this wonderful privilege of sharing the Dharma.

Birth

This is the first of the four sufferings listed in the Buddhist teachings. It refers to living in this world as a human being and what it means to be human and the discomfort associated with living and experiencing the world. We are born into the ocean of birth and death, samsara. *Jodo Shinshu is essentially teaching us how to swim.*

Teriyaki Priest

◆ ◆ ◆

Good thoughts arise in us through the prompting of good karma from the past, and evil comes to be thought and performed through the working of evil karma. The late Master said, "Know that every evil act done—even as slight as a particle on the tip of a strand of rabbit's fur or sheep's wool—has its cause in past karma."

Tannisho, Chapter 13, *Collected Works of Shinran (CWS)*, p. 670

I peeked into the *hondo* to see why the lights had been left on and what was making the strange clucking sounds. Upon opening the door, I was assaulted by a strange yet familiar smell. It wasn't the perfumed smell of incense or the various flowers upon the altar, but the distinct smell of barbecued teriyaki chicken. Opening the door all the way, I saw to my astonishment hundreds—maybe thousands—of crying, clucking chickens, seated throughout the hondo.

The altar had been set up for a funeral service. Set before the altar, rather than a casket, was a huge gold *imari* plate, piled high with our temple's teriyaki chicken. Carefully arranged around the glistening pieces of flesh were small white carnations. A gasp slipped from my mouth. The hondo was suddenly silent and all the chickens looked in my direction. Suddenly a loud voice came from the altar: "Human, come forward and learn about suffering!"

Fear streamed through my body. My mind raced, "Teriyaki chicken…chickens in the hondo…learn about suffering!" Was I going to become teriyaki priest? No matter how my mind tried to resist, my feet kept moving me toward the front of the hondo. I could feel the sweat begin to stream down the sides of my face, sticky and warm like teriyaki sauce. Clearing the sweat from my eyes, I saw there was a very

3

large chicken standing at the podium where I usually stood. To my surprise he began to speak to me in English, not chicken. He sounded like the Wizard of Oz when he commanded Dorothy to come forward. This powerful wizard of the chickens was commanding me, "Come forward, human. I want you to learn about existential suffering. I have heard you tell your Sangha about suffering, but do you really understand the depth of suffering you and your fellow humans cause not only to yourselves, but to all of us sentient beings?"

As this chicken in robes spoke, there was a loud ruffling of feathers and a few harsh shrieks from the chickens that had now begun to form a circle around the plate of teriyaki chicken and me. I thought, "I knew I should have dieted; then I wouldn't look so appealing as teriyaki priest."

"I..I...didn't know—" I squeaked and pleaded to the group. "Fool! Shut up!" shouted the large robed chicken. "How many times have you used the term 'sentient beings'? How many times have you spoken to your Sangha about the nature of suffering and the life of gratitude? How can you say, 'I didn't know—' so pathetically? WE ARE SENTIENT BEINGS, HUMAN! DO NOT PLEAD IGNORANCE. You insult us with your babbling, 'I don't know—' SPEAK TO HIM, BROTHERS AND SISTERS!"

A large speckled chicken fluttered toward the front of the other fowl and spoke, "Throughout your temples of the Buddhist Churches of America, hundreds of thousands—maybe millions—of our parents, grandparents, children and grandchildren have been sacrificed to keep your temples going. Yes, we have been sacrificed so that you and your Sangha could listen to the Dharma. You have been blessed to be born into human life. Do you realize the meaning of the Threefold Refuge, 'Hard is it to be born into human life'?"

"Yes, yes, I am grateful for being born into human life," I pleaded with the fluttering crowd.

"Shut up and let her continue, HUMAN!" came a cluck from the crowd.

"We chickens understand that the Dharma is truth and that to be born a chicken means that many of us will end up as food for your bazaars, Obons and various fundraisers. We can only hope that our sacrifice for the temple is better than ending up merely a bucket of Kentucky Fried, or worse, a chicken nugget. At least our children die for a worthy cause—the Dharma. But for you to blubber out 'I didn't know—' makes me sick. You, a Buddhist priest, should at least recognize the countless millions of us that have been sacrificed for you and yours to listen to the Dharma. We should peck the ears off your head if that is all the gratitude you have."

With her words, I could feel the chickens moving in closer to me. "COCK-A-DOODLE-DOO!" screamed some of the more aggressive roosters. "Let's peck out his eyes!" shrieked one of the chickens. "Henny Penny!" shouted the chicken priest. "Calm down, all of you. Henny Penny, remember what happened the last time you got all worked up about the sky falling?" That seemed to settle them down a little.

"We won't hurt you, human. Nor do we expect that you will change the manner of your fundraising. We just want you to understand that it isn't only the physical labor of your temple members or the donations that you receive that allow you to hear the Dharma.

"We know that there are members of your Sangha who do not understand that to listen to the Dharma and to receive *shinjin* is of primary importance. They feel that merely working at the bazaars and various activities is good enough and that that is Buddhism or being Buddhist. However, we want them to know that our sacrifice is not merely for cultural traditions. For example, Obon is not a folk tradition. It is an opportunity to hear the Dharma! We do not want to die for a folk tradition. We are not sacrificing our lives just for you to have a good time. We give our lives in gratitude for you humans to have the opportunity to hear the Dharma. Listen, please listen. That is all that we ask." I could only bow my head and say, "Namo Amida Butsu."

The large priest and the Sangha seemed to settle down with my recitation of the Nembutsu. "Good, we know that you humans are weak. Yet we are willing to accept our lot as chickens for you to gain the value of the Dharma. I hope that you will try to let your Sangha know our feelings."

"Thank you, Sensei, I will try to explain what I can." The chicken priest clucked and nodded with the others that were clucking seemingly in agreement. I suddenly found myself sitting in my office with a translation of the *Tannisho* opened to Chapter 13. It must have been a dream! However, I still can't explain the chicken feathers stuck to the soles of my shoes. Namo Amida Butsu.

The Curious Birth of Siddhartha

◆ ◆ ◆

Is it so small a thing
To have enjoy'd the sun,
To have lived light in the spring,
To have loved, to have thought, to have done;
To have advanced true friends, and beat down baffling foes—

That we must feign a bliss
Of doubtful future date,
And, while we dream on this,
Lose all our present state,
And relegate to worlds yet distant our repose?

Matthew Arnold, "Empedocles on Etna"

This month we will be celebrating Hanamatsuri. Hanamatsuri literally means "flower festival." The flowers are in reference to the flowers that were said to have suddenly blossomed at the birth of Siddhartha Gautama, whom we also call Shakyamuni Buddha. In this mythical birth scene, dragons fly down from the heavens to assist in the birth of the Buddha. They carry the child to the Earth as he leaves the womb of Queen Maya. Sweet rain begins to fall, nourishing the Earth. The Earth as witness shakes in six directions and begins to blossom with flowers. The baby Siddhartha is said to have walked seven steps and announced to the world, "In the heavens above and the world below, I alone am the World Honored One."

This story of the birth of the human child Siddhartha Gautama, who would become the historical Buddha, should not be taken literally. Yet I do not think it should easily be dismissed as a foolish fairy tale, either. Throughout human history, mankind has needed to embellish stories that are important. When I think of the birth of my own children, in my mind's eye, it was an incredibly beautiful moment. To the nurses and doctor who delivered them, it was probably just another birth that they very likely won't even remember.

For me, their birth was the fulfillment of my life dream. Their birth seemed to answer the question I had struggled with for years: Why am I here? or What is the meaning of my life? In this story, I remember the angels dressed in white bringing forth my children. The tears of joy in my eyes felt as though they were moistened with sweet rain that seemed to have fallen from the sky. My world, my life, my existence, were shaken into true meaning and existence at the moment of their birth. Yet very little of this was caught on the video taken when they were born. To the casual observer, there were no angels, the Earth didn't shake and there was no rain falling in the delivery room. Yet which version is the true version?

In each of our lives there needs to be truth and objectivity. The Buddhism I have learned and am trying to explain is a religion without superstition. I would argue with my friends who are Theravada monks as to the actual facts of the birth of Siddhartha. Yet, I can also listen to this story and understand why we celebrate Hanamatsuri. I, too, can see the flowers blooming.

The passage at the beginning of this essay is from the poem, "Empedocles on Etna" by Matthew Arnold. It is a very long poem, but I love this passage that asks whether or not these things in our life are enough: to have enjoyed the sun; to have lived light in the spring; to have loved, to have thought, to have done; to have advanced true friends, and beat down baffling foes. When stated as Arnold does in this poem, I would say yes, this is the beauty of life. It isn't necessary to dream of a future afterlife. The miracle of this life should be enough. This world as we see and experience it is Truth and need not be embellished with superstitions and fantastic stories.

However, as a human being I have a need to be reminded that there is more than just meets the eye. Even with all I receive, my *bonno* (greed, anger, ignorance) says I want more. To just live and appreciate all that I have should be enough. Issa beautifully stated, "The world of dew is the world of dew, and yet, and yet—" I do forget about the beauty of the spring sun as soon as the evening comes. I take for granted so much that life has given me. Issa's "and yet, and yet—" goes beyond Arnold's allusion to just this world. This unseen beauty beyond superstition can only be "Namo Amida Butsu." With the Nembutsu I appreciate it all, and it is enough. In this world of black and white, the Nembutsu changes everything to color. Happy Hanamatsuri! Namo Amida Butsu!

The Magic Mirror

◆ ◆ ◆

The True intention of the Tathagata in coming to this world is to present the truth of the Original Vow. This preaching is extremely difficult to comprehend and is revealed just like the Udumbara lotus flower.

Daikyo Wasan

Once upon a time there were two very special children, each born to very special parents at a very special time, place and day. The circumstances in which they were born were created especially for them. The entire universe awaited their birth and when they were born. It was as if the entire universe greeted them.

One child's mother and father doted on him night and day. When he was hungry, he would cry. When he was tired, he would cry. When he didn't get his way, he would cry. His cry would bring his parents running to pick him up and do whatever they could to make him comfortable. His parents and family all loved this little boy dearly, even though it seemed as if nothing they could do would make him happy.

As this child grew, the conditions of his childhood were what most of us might call "fit for a king." You would think that a child born to such a family would be truly happy; but not this child. Nothing seemed to make this little prince happy. The more his parents gave, the more he wanted. He was never satisfied.

One day his father said, "Your mom and I knew that you wanted a Nintendo video game. But we thought you would like the new Super NES system. Since this system is new, we thought you should also have a new large screen TV and a stereo video system to go with it. We hope you'll enjoy it, son."

The little boy's reply was, "Now my room looks small. The stereo speakers are too close together and I can't hear the separation."

The mother and father were a little disappointed that their gift had saddened their child. They told him he could have their room since it was bigger. Rather than thank his parents, he suggested that building him a special room might work better than their bedroom.

The parents looked at one another and promised they would do their best. The boy shouted, "Well, until then, hurry and move my things into your room. I guess I'll just have to make do with it until you make my new video room!"

On the other side of town, the other child's life was not so blessed. She was born into a very poor family. Her mother and father could not even afford to raise her and left her near the entryway of the neighborhood market. When this child cried and cried, there was no one to answer her cries. Finally, a patrol car noticed the old shopping cart she had been left in and upon investigating found the little girl, wrapped in some old newspapers and a worn-out bedspread.

The child was placed in a state orphanage. As she grew, the few playthings available were to be shared by all the children in the orphanage. The clothes she wore had been donated to the various shelters and welfare agencies throughout the city. When she awoke in the middle of the night, there was no one to answer her cries. She wondered if she would ever find someone who would love her.

One day she asked one of the attendants at the orphanage, "Do you think my parents will ever come back for me?" Without saying anything, the attendant gave her an embarrassed smile and walked away. All stories that begin with "Once upon a time," should have a little magic, and this story is no different.

On their 12th birthdays, both of these children born under very different circumstances each received a mysterious present. The little boy snarled, "I know it's not the radio-controlled helicopter I asked for. It's way too small." Upon ripping open the package he angrily shouted, "Is this some sort of joke?"

"No, honey, it's a magic mirror. We met this man on the street and he told us that if you look into the mirror, it will tell you all you need to know to become a true and real human being. Just take a look," his mother said.

"What other present did you get me?" asked the boy.

"Please, son, just take a look. It's supposed to be magic," said the father.

"All right, but you still owe me."

The little boy picked up the mirror and to his surprise, instead of seeing himself, he saw a ferocious, repulsive face looking back at him. The face staring back was bloated with red eyes that darted back and forth like a reptile searching for its next meal. The mouth was very small and puckered with large, almost translucent, blistered lips. The size of the mouth belied the size of the lips, for the mouth would barely accommodate a grain of rice. The little boy was so shocked that he couldn't say a word. The only sound was of his soiling his shorts.

He was turning to throw the mirror at his mother when a loud, regal voice bellowed from the mirror, "You are a spoiled, selfish little brat who has absolutely no consideration for the feelings of others. You have a loving family that you take advantage of. Your parents give you everything they can and yet you ask for more. This world is yours, but you must learn gratitude. This image in the mirror is you! Without a heart of gratitude you are nothing more than what you see in the mirror. Your only chance to change yourself is to become a true and real being of gratitude. Your parents cannot help you with this. It is solely up to you!" The boy was speechless. No one had ever spoken to him this way. He had never had to really look at himself or consider his behavior.

On the other side of town, the little girl was returning home from school when a man in a purple suit approached her.

"GET AWAY FROM ME!" she screamed.

"Don't be afraid. I'm not going to hurt you and I only want to give you this magical mirror."

"What do you think I am! Just because I'm poor doesn't mean I'm stupid. Even at the orphanage they teach us about perverts like you."

"I'll leave this mirror on the ground. You can decide for yourself whether to pick it up or leave it. This is not just any mirror, but one that will show you both how to be a true and real being of gratitude and the way to happiness." As he placed the mirror on the ground, he faded away.

The little girl stood there in amazement. Was this man her fairy godfather? She had never believed in those fairy tales that were read to the children on weekends by a volunteer. But she had seen that man with her own eyes. She had heard him speak to her with her own ears. She wondered, "Could that mirror really tell me the path to happiness? Nothing has ever gone right for me. My own mother and father didn't even want me. I wonder what that man really meant about being a true and real human being?"

She cautiously walked up to the mirror, picked it up and looked in. To her surprise she saw a little princess looking back at her. She was so startled she dropped the mirror and a very clear, reassuring voice came from the mirror: "Don't be afraid, and pick me up." She felt a quiet assurance glow within herself. She picked up the mirror and once again saw the little princess looking back at her. As she looked closer, she realized that she herself was the princess in the mirror.

Just as she made this startling realization, the man's voice calmly spoke through the mirror: "This world is yours, my dear. At times it may seem that you have been treated unfairly. However, we live in a world that is not always fair. There is birth, old age, sickness and death and all things are impermanent. Just be true to yourself. The entire universe has waited for your birth and welcomes you with open arms. What you do with your life is up to you. Remember that you are an important part of this world. Trust in yourself and live in gratitude that the world is here for you, and you will find happiness."

The little girl looked at herself and nothing seemed to have changed. She was still wearing the same old dress and dirty socks and shoes, but something did seem different. Something inside her had changed, or rather blossomed. She realized that the mirror was truly magic. From that day forward she lived her life with a new confidence and shared the mirror with all the children in the orphanage.

This is the end of this little fable of the magic mirror, and like most fables and fairy tales, it has a happy ending. However, in truth, whether an ending is happy is totally up to the children reading the story. This magic mirror is the same as the Buddha's teachings. The teachings of the Buddha are to show us who we truly are. The magic of the Buddha's teachings can only have meaning through your own life and what you choose to do with it. We are all born as very special, lucky people, although there are times when that may seem hard to believe. As with the little girl, to be able to see the truth sometimes requires a little magic of a good Dharma friend. In this way, we may all live happily ever after. Namo Amida Butsu.

Hometown Love

◆◆◆

I admire those cold, proud beings who adventure upon the paths of great and daemonic beauty and despise 'mankind'; but I do not envy them. For if anything is capable of making a poet of a literary man, it is my hometown love of the human, the living and ordinary. All warmth derives from this love, all kindness and humor.

Thomas Mann, *Tonio Kröger*

As Buddhists living in America, we are often placed by society and ourselves in the position of having to defend our beliefs. In many ways this can be beneficial, for the need to defend our beliefs often makes us stronger. However, there are some Buddhists who feel a need to apologize for their beliefs. This is something I feel is totally unnecessary and detrimental to Buddhism, and in the long run, to one's self.

I can think of no reason that one should be embarrassed about the Buddhist teachings. Within Buddhism we find one of the most non-judgmental, compassionate teachings in the history of mankind. The historical Buddha Shakyamuni has said, "There are 84,000 paths to enlightenment." What he means by 84,000 paths is that there is an infinite number of ways to awaken to Truth.

All of us human beings are individuals, consisting of our own histories and various causes and conditions which make up our lives. We each have our own stories and truths that make us who we are. Buddhism recognizes that the teachings must be flexible to encompass so many different viewpoints. There cannot be only one true and real teaching, just as there cannot be only one story or history to identify each and every one of us.

Buddhism is nothing more than a finger pointing out our way. There is the famous Zen painting of a man laughing and pointing at the moon. If we focus on the man's finger, we can see that he is laughing at us. Focusing upon his finger is narrowing our minds. In addition, that finger is his, not ours. The man is telling us to open our minds and look at the moon. The moon shines upon each and every one of us, in our own place and time. To see its true beauty, we must view it from our own perspective. We should open our eyes to the light shining down upon us. If we are able to honestly see what the light is revealing, we may laugh with him, for the light reveals our true selves. If we cannot accept and laugh at our own true selves, we are in serious trouble.

I would like to write about some of the basics of the Buddhist teachings. In writing, I am not telling you that this is the definitive Buddhist way. I am merely explaining to you what I have found to be the beauty of the Buddhist teachings. I am writing as a third generation Japanese American married male, who was born and raised in Salt Lake City, Utah. As an ordained Jodo Shinshu Buddhist priest, my views are interpreted from that particular perspective because it cannot be otherwise. However, I hope that you will find that although each of us is different, in many ways, as human beings we are very much alike. I hope that you will find some teaching that will enlighten your way to look at yourself and maybe laugh a little at our human frailties. Whenever possible I will try to use passages from Western philosophers and thinkers rather than famous Buddhist philosophers and thinkers. I want to show that Jodo Shinshu is speaking about basic truths in life that transcend the boundaries of culture and race; this means they can be found in many different places, not only in Buddhist texts and literature.

I began this essay with the passage by Thomas Mann because I believe that one of the problems many of us find in our Buddhist teachings is that when we identify ourselves as Buddhists, we seem to set ourselves apart from the larger society we are born into. I was born and raised in Salt Lake City, a predominantly white, Christian society. Identifying myself as a Buddhist and a Japanese American Buddhist priest seems to set me apart from this society. Yet who and what I am has been defined by this society I was born into. This is my hometown love. This is where I first discovered people and life. If I were to reject this society that I was born into, am I not rejecting a part of who I am? I feel that we must accept the society we are born into as a part of ourselves. No one fits into society perfectly. Even if I were born a white, male Mormon, descended from Brigham Young, I could not consider myself a perfect fit.

Each of us develops a particular perception of the world. Steve Young, the quarterback for the San Francisco '49ers, is a rich, famous Brigham Young University graduate with a law degree. However, as of the writing of this article, he is in his early 30s, but not married with children. Most Mormon males are married with children by the time they are his age. There is no perfect fit. Each of us is flawed in some way when we try to compare ourselves to some societal standard. Coming to accept and understand our own flawed nature is the beginning of understanding Jodo Shinshu. As the philosopher Meister Eckhart wrote, "To get at the core of God at his greatest, one must first get into the core of himself at his least."

In Jodo Shinshu, one of the first steps we must realize is how imperfect we are. This is why Buddhism says "Life is suffering." It is through our imperfection and understanding that imperfection that we can find healing and joy. The philosopher-psychologist William James called it "torn-to-pieces-hood," his translation of the German *Zerrissenheit*. As human beings, each of us experiences this feeling of being torn asunder—being pulled by various forces of family, job, marriage, etc. Yet if we are able to step back for a moment, we will realize that each of these forces is what identifies who we are. It is living in this world.

Look at baseball, as an example. If you were able to successfully hit safely in 4 out of 10 at-bats, you would probably be a millionaire all-star player. Basketball superstar Michael Jordan has said, "I've failed over and over again in my life. And that is why I succeed." We can look at life in the same way. Jodo Shinshu teaches us how to deal with failure. We should learn from a young age that in life, failure is just part of the game. We can accept and understand this basic fact of life by understanding this being-torn-apartness. We can see how we are being embraced and healed at the same time. This is the core of the Buddhist teaching. It is not a pessimistic, nihilistic teaching as some would claim. It is a teaching that accepts us as we are and shows us how to understand that imperfections make us truly human, and to face ourselves squarely, seeing ourselves as we are: mixed up, paradoxical, incomplete, not quite fitting in.

This teaching is not something new or different. It is not just the Jodo Shinshu way. The Delphic Oracle's first admonition was "Know thyself." As the Lizensker Rebbe, one of the founding leaders of the Hasidic movement, said, "Only God is perfect. Man's actions must be basically defective in part. If one believes his good deed or my study to be thoroughly pure and perfect, this is a sure sign that they are thoroughly bad." These comments from Greece, Poland and the United States are all basic rules for playing the game of *life*. Jodo Shinshu is one of the ways for us to understand this, our *life*.

Touch of Tradition

◆ ◆ ◆

Pure Land Buddhism traditionally emphasizes the way of life in each era. That is to say, the teaching of Amida Buddha's Primal Vow must be translated into the emerging context of each new age. We see this process in the writings of Shinran Shonin.... Shinran's successors have also striven to interpret the teachings for their times.... Even in Japan at present, the concrete expressions of Buddhist truth...need to be translated and adapted to the contemporary context.

Koshin Otani

The candles from the altar lighted the hall as all the supplicants knelt with their heads bowed to the ground and their right hand palms up.

Ever so slowly you could hear movement from the rear of the *naijin*. It was the sound of tradition. The Zenmon, retired Gomonshu (Abbot) of Jodo Shinshu Hongwanji-ha, was entering the hall to begin the ordination of my class. I could hear the slight swish of his elaborate robes brushing together as he walked from person to person, placing a pinch of the ceremonial incense into the palm of our hand.

I am sure that many images and thoughts raced through each person's mind. This was the culmination of our ten days of separation from everyday life. We had each gone through a series of tests and rituals in preparation for this first step as priests of Jodo Shinshu Hongwanji-ha.

I have heard a number of moving accounts from my fellow priests of their experience during this *Tokudo* ordination. To be honest, all I could think of was the pain in my knees. I had injured my knees during the hours of sitting in *seiza* during the various classes and rituals. I was lucky that Rev. David Matsumoto had brought me a case of instant ice packs so that nightly I could tape them to my knees to bring the swelling down.

For many of my fellow priests, this moment with the spiritual head of our sect of Buddhism walking from the altar to anoint us with incense was one of the extreme highlights of their becoming priests. However, all I could think was, "I bet if the Gomonshu and not his retired father were performing our Tokudo, I wouldn't have to kneel here so long!" Although there is a tinge of guilt in not feeling the ominous presence of hundreds of years of religious tradition, in this ritual ordination, all I could think about were my knees and how much longer is this ceremony going to last?

Since that time, I would talk with my fellow priests and many were indeed aware of all the causes and conditions that had led up to that very moment. My friend, Rev. Gustavo Pinto from Brazil, recounted how overwhelmed with emotion he felt by the beauty and tradition of the Tokudo ceremony. However, a couple of my close friends made me feel better when they told me that after the Gomonshu had placed the incense in their hands, all they could think about was having to dirty their beautiful new robes by rubbing the incense into it. I guess some of us aren't quite so sensitive to tradition.

On March 19, 1999, our temple and district were fortunate to have had a visitation by Gomonshu Koshin Otani, the 24th generation descendant of Shinran Shonin, the founder of Jodo Shinshu. To tell you the truth, it was one of the most stressful days since I had become a *Kaikyoshi* (overseas minister) 12 years earlier. The night before his visitation I could barely sleep. I kept wondering if everything had been taken care of. What do I say to him? How do I act? Will there be people coming to the temple for his visit? Etc., etc.

Those of you who were able to join us know that everything turned out beautifully. I was extremely proud of our temple and the Sangha. I would especially like to thank Paul and Kathy Terashima, Jane Sakashita, Lynn Shimada, Reiko Watanabe and Brenda Koga for all their help during his visitation. We could never have had such a successful visitation without their help.

There were a little over 100 members who greeted the Gomonshu. Many of our Dharma school students also attended. The Gomonshu and our Bishop Watanabe commented on how nice it was to see all the children, especially on a school day. I feel that having Bishop Watanabe present helped make the Gomonshu's visitation so enjoyable. Of all the things that are said about our Bishop, the one thing that is evident to everyone who meets him is that he is extremely friendly and personable. He treats everyone like an old friend.

While the Gomonshu was having tea and dessert with all of us, Bishop Watanabe told me to tell people to come up and greet the Gomonshu. I asked if they could take pictures. Bishop Watanabe said, "Sure, sure. This is a very good chance for people to meet him. That is why he's here." Many people had the chance to go up, shake hands and take pictures with him. This type of personal contact is almost unheard of in Japan.

To give an example, when I was in Japan as a student, a classmate of mine asked a few of us if we could help him at his temple, since the Gomonshu would be visiting. I didn't think that it was that big a deal. I was very surprised at how big a deal it was. My friend's temple is in the middle of Osaka, so the streets near his temple are very narrow. The car that was bringing the Gomonshu could not fit through the streets. Therefore, a red carpet was rented or purchased to run the three or more blocks that the Gomonshu would be walking to get to the temple.

As the Gomonshu walked, an attendant carrying a large red umbrella walked behind him, shading him as he went. My classmates and I were near the entrance to the temple. As he passed us, he glanced over and gave a slight bow of acknowledgment. After he passed, I heard a whimpering sound next to me. Looking over, I saw one of my classmates crying. I asked her what was wrong, thinking that maybe the Gomonshu or his attendant had stepped on her toe or something. She replied, "It's just so overwhelming. I never thought I would get so close to the Gomonshu; and then he looked over and nodded to us. I'm so happy I can't help but cry. I have to call my mother tonight and tell her."

I chuckled to myself and we continued with his visitation. My friend's temple had all sorts of special commemorative items created for the Gomonshu's visit. The members of his temple were presented with these things. For these members of this temple in Osaka, this was truly a once-in-a-lifetime opportunity. However, they could not even imagine going up and shaking hands with him, as we had done.

Our bishop is exceptional in creating an atmosphere that allows the members to feel comfortable. On talking with a few of the Gomonshu's entourage of attendants, I asked them how they felt. They all mentioned the extreme stress they had felt when traveling with the Gomonshu. I asked them what they talked to the Gomonshu about. They looked at me in surprise, "We do not talk to the Gomonshu except to answer if he asks us something."

I said, "You mean even after traveling with him like this you don't talk?" They said the only person they have even met who seemed comfortable around the Gomonshu was Bishop Watanabe. Even Bishop Fujikawa, a governor of Hongwanji, seemed stressed when in the presence of the Gomonshu.

I felt relieved that during the banquet I was sitting at the head table, with Bishop Watanabe between the Gomonshu and myself. I asked the Bishop something about the Gomonshu and he leaned back in his chair and said, "Just ask him yourself." He tapped the Gomonshu and said, "Rev. Hirano wants to ask you something." At first I was a little flustered, but as the Gomonshu began to speak, I soon realized he was a human being just like the rest of us.

He talked about skiing in Japan and said that his son was on a skiing trip to Hokkaido. I mentioned that our Dharma school was having a ski trip at the end of the month. Jokingly I said, "You're welcome to join us." He smiled and softly replied, "I wish I could." As he said this, I could see in his eyes that he really meant it.

Our Gomonshu was a man with the same types of feelings and emotions that each of us has. As he spoke of his children, I could feel the same bonds of parental love that all of us feel for our own children. I am sure he missed his family. He spoke of attending the Centennial of BCA this coming August and said that his family would be with him. I could tell that this would be a very special chance for him.

I realized that here was a man who was born into a centuries-old tradition. Whether or not he wanted to fill this position, he was now carrying it out for the benefit of Jodo Shinshu. He was an example of the living Nembutsu teachings, started by Shinran Shonin over 700 years earlier. Whether or not we support such traditions in America, it is important that we understand them and what their place holds for us. I began this article with a passage from the opening address given by the Gomonshu at an international convention on Jodo Shinshu studies at Harvard a number of years ago:

Pure Land Buddhism traditionally emphasizes the way of life in each era. That is to say, the teaching of Amida Buddha's Primal Vow must be translated into the emerging context of each new age. We see this process in the writings of Shinran Shonin.... Shinran's successors have also striven to interpret the teachings for their times.... Even in Japan at present, the concrete expressions of Buddhist truth...need to be translated and adapted to the contemporary context.

As the Gomonshu says, "Shinran's successors have also striven to interpret the teachings for their times." We each had a chance to touch a part of our Jodo Shinshu tradition. As a result of my chance to converse with the Gomonshu, I was allowed to see how although we may come from different worlds and societies, we are one within the Nembutsu. All the rituals and ceremonies of Hongwanji would not allow me this insight. It was through the opportunities created by the Gomonshu and Bishop Watanabe and the hard work of our temple members that I was able to understand how real the Nembutsu is.

The Nembutsu we call out in gratitude in Salt Lake City, Utah, is the same as that of the Gomonshu of Jodo Shinshu Hongwanji-ha. It is up to each of us to understand the Primal Vow of Amida Buddha for our age, time and place. It is my hope that we can and will continue to do this. However, it is not by throwing out the traditions of the past, but by understanding their deeper meaning and connections to our present lives. Thank you once again for showing that the Nembutsu teaching is alive and well in Salt Lake City and that we have a wonderful temple and Sangha. Namo Amida Butsu.

Why I Am a Jodo Shinshu Buddhist

◆ ◆ ◆

This, then, is the true teaching, easy to practice for small, foolish beings; it is the straight way, easy to traverse for the dull and ignorant. Among all the teachings the Great Sage preached in his lifetime, none surpasses this ocean of virtues. Let the one who seeks to abandon the defiled and aspire for the pure; who is confused in practice and vacillating in faith; whose mind is dark and whose understanding deficient; whose evils are heavy and whose karmic obstructions manifold—let such persons embrace above all the Tathagata's exhortations, take refuge without fail in the most excellent direct path, devote themselves solely to this practice, and revere only this shinjin.

Preface to *Kyogyoshinsho, CWS*, pp. 3-4

Our temples in the Buddhist Churches of America and our temples in Salt Lake City and Ogden are undergoing a change. It is evident that the Nisei (second generation Japanese Americans) who developed the organizational structure of our temples are dying out. The average age of the Nisei is probably in the early 80's. The Sansei (third generation Japanese Americans) are in their 50's and 60's.

Our temples are also beginning to have many non-Japanese who do not come to the temple for cultural activities. The language spoken at our temple is 99% English. The economic level of the average temple member is probably in the middle class. The average educational level of our temple members is probably at least that of a college graduate. The majority of our members also attend the temple as families.

With the exception of our members attending the temple as families, there has been quite a change in the composition of the Sangha over the past 100 years of our temple. Yes, in 2012, our temple will be celebrating 100 years in Utah. Originally, our members and the minister were Japanese-speaking. There were very few if any non-Japanese attending the temple. As much as for religious and spiritual sustenance, the temple was a gathering place for the entire Japanese community for secular reasons. As I have explained in previous articles, the temple was the guardian of a Japanese culture that the Issei (first generation) hoped would be passed on to their children. I believe much of the culture of the temple has changed over the past 100 years. However, the reason we are Jodo Shinshu Buddhist has not.

Speaking from a very personal level, since the time I was a Dharma school student here, the religious climate of Utah has also changed. When I was a child, most of my friends had no idea what a Buddhist was. In Salt Lake, Buddhism could only be found at our temple and the smaller Nichiren temple. When the television show *Kung Fu* began in 1972, many people thought that all Buddhists must know martial arts.

It was about this time that we began to hear about Zen Buddhism in popular culture. Robert Pirsig's *Zen and the Art of Motorcycle Maintenance* was published in 1974. Although there began to be English books on Buddhism in the 60's, such as Phillip Kapleau's *Three Pillars of Zen*, Pirsig's book and the television show *Kung Fu* seemed to announce the arrival of Buddhism into the realm of popular culture. It was during the 70's that the Tibetan Buddhists began to teach in the United States.

It was a nice change when America and the culture around me began to appreciate that Buddhism was a legitimate religion. I had attended various Christian churches with my friends, but many of their ideas didn't appeal to me. I also had two sets of friends: one group was from my neighborhood; the other group was the kids I had met at the temple. As I got older, it became more obvious that I was different from my neighborhood friends since I wasn't planning to go on a mission. When I went to the university, most of my neighborhood friends had gone on missions. So the friendships I developed at the temple became my primary friendships in college.

In college, as I began to explore my identity, I realized that much of the ethics or morality I had developed over the years was from things I had learned at the temple. Ideas such as the impermanence of life, karma and humility were the ideas that formed my own personal identity. Yet, I wasn't comfortable with expressing what Buddhism was. What was Buddhism? Why were people suddenly interested in what the Buddha taught?

I went to the Institute of Buddhist Studies to find out exactly what Buddhism was. I learned about Theravada Buddhism, Zen Buddhism, Shingon Buddhism and a variety of Japanese forms of Buddhism. What I found was that Theravada Buddhism was a difficult, highly disciplined path that one could fully realize only after leaving the life of a householder and becoming a monk.

I had no intention of giving up sex and a variety of other things to become enlightened. Shingon Buddhism was much too mystical for my taste. Performing a myriad of rituals to better understand the truth of this life was not something I could do. Zen Buddhism, although it has changed in America, required a great deal of time sitting in meditation. It was also a form of monastic Buddhism and it required that I find a particular teacher to guide me. I didn't know much about Tibetan Buddhism; however, I knew that it required much more study than I was willing to give.

As I read more about Jodo Shinshu and the way Shinran had spent years in meditation and study, later abandoning them for the Nembutsu practice, I realized that this was the only path that I was reasonably fit to follow. Shinran believed that enlightenment and nirvana were not secret or extremely difficult practices. It was about accepting oneself as a *bombu* (foolish being) and having a belief in the compassion of the universe (Amida Buddha) as the way to enlightenment.

After studying many other religions, I knew without a doubt I was a foolish being. I knew that I was confused in practice and had questions of faith. My mind was dark and I was deficient in many things. I also knew that I had committed a variety of things in my life that would be called heavy evil and karmic obstructions. As the preface to the *Kyogyoshinsho* states:

> This, then, is the true teaching easy to practice for small, foolish beings; it is the straight way easy to traverse for the dull and ignorant. Among all the teachings the Great Sage preached in his lifetime, none surpasses this ocean of virtues. Let the one who seeks to abandon the defiled and aspire for the pure; who is confused in practice and vacillating in faith; whose mind is dark and whose understanding deficient; whose evils are heavy and whose karmic obstructions manifold—let such persons embrace above all the Tathagata's exhortations, take refuge without fail in the most excellent direct path, devote themselves solely to this practice, and revere only this shinjin.

Shinran was basically telling me that Jodo Shinshu was the path for a person like me.

It is wonderful that the religious climate in Utah has become more open. It is a blessing that our temples have opened up and our Sangha has moved on to be a part of American culture. However, I have been surprised by a few members who look toward other forms of Buddhism and express a type of infatuation with there being more non-Japanese following them than Jodo Shinshu. It is as if they feel that, since non-Japanese Americans are following Zen or Tibetan Buddhism, these forms must have something our teachings do not.

I hope that they will begin to study what it is that Jodo Shinshu has before they become too discouraged. I encourage them to try Zen or try the Tibetan form of Buddhism, if they want to wear robes. However, if they believe that Jodo Shinshu is not sufficient to fulfill their personal needs and desires, they must ask themselves, "Why am I Jodo Shinshu?" I think it is a great place to start. Namo Amida Butsu.

Traditional Jodo Shinshu Meditation?

Reverently contemplating Amida's directing of virtue for our going forth to the Pure Land, I find that there is great practice, there is great shinjin. The great practice is to say the Name of the Tathagatha of unhindered light.

The great practice, embodying all good acts and possessing all roots of virtue, is perfect and most rapid in bringing them to fullness. It is the treasure ocean of virtues that is suchness or true reality. For this reason, it is called great practice.

Kyogyoshinsho, Chapter on Practice, *CWS*, Vol. 1, p. 13

These passages reveal that saying the Name breaks through all the ignorance of sentient beings and fulfills all their aspirations. Saying the Name is the right act, supreme, true, and excellent. The right act is the nembutsu. The nembutsu is Namu-amida-butsu. Namu-amida-butsu is right-minded-ness. Let this be known.

Kyogyoshinsho, Chapter on Practice, *CWS,* Vol. 1, pp. 17-18

I had written most of this article a few years back when we first began our meditation services, led by Carmela. Since a new committee of the BCA called Minister's Training and Development was formed, which I am part of, the question of meditation in our BCA temples is once again being addressed. There are some who have tried to implement it and others who are against having it in their temples. The reason for not having it is usually because it isn't a traditional part of our temples. I would like to share my feelings concerning this so-called traditional approach to meditation in our temples.

Traditionally in Jodo Shinshu Buddhism, when we refer to practice, we look to the portions of Shinran Shonin's *Kyogyoshinsho,* "Chapter on Practice," with which I began this essay. In essence, Shinran is establishing that the great practice is the practice accomplished and fulfilled by the Bodhisattva Dharmakara in becoming Amida Buddha. We are thus the recipients of the merits from this great practice. Amida Buddha has completed these vows, and the subsequent merits resulting from their completion has provided us foolish beings with a path to enlightenment.

This path to enlightenment is the saying of the name, "Namo Amida Butsu." Therefore, all other forms of practice are unnecessary for our goal of enlightenment. Only the saying of the name is necessary.

Since we have been given this Vow by the Tathagatha, we can take any occasion in daily life for saying the Name and need not wait to recite it at the very end of life; we should simply give ourselves up totally to the entrusting with sincere mind of the Tathagata. When persons realize this true and real shinjin, they enter completely into the compassionate light that grasps, never to abandon, and hence become established in the stage of the truly settled.

Notes on the Inscriptions on Sacred Scrolls,
CWS, Vol. 1, p. 494

"To be established in the stage of the truly settled" refers to the stage in a person's journey where without doubt they will attain Buddhahood. Therefore, in a traditional sense, the practice of sitting meditation that is found in almost all other sects of Buddhism is not included as part of a traditional Jodo Shinshu service. In referring to traditional services, I mean burning incense, to purify and remind us of our interdependence; bowing and reciting the Nembutsu as part of the burning of the incense; chanting the sutras, to praise the virtues of Buddha; and beginning and ending services with the recitation of the Nembutsu. It is also important to include a Dharma Talk. These are all standard features of the Jodo Shinshu service. Whether you are in a Jodo Shinshu temple in the United States or Japan, most of these elements are a part of the service.

However, the important element that Shinran emphasizes is the Nembutsu. In our services, the Nembutsu is something that is a sort of call-and-respond type of practice. The minister or leader says "Namo Amida Butsu" and the Sangha responds with "Namo Amida Butsu." This type of Nembutsu is only done in BCA, Canada or Hawaii. Shinran never suggested this type of practice. However, it is done almost without hesitation in our BCA temples.

In Jodo Shinshu our practice is often defined as listening to the Dharma (*monpo*). Each of these elements of our standard service is more than just listening with our ears. I remember when I was in Japan, I struggled with the Japanese language. During one lecture, just as I was feeling somewhat confident in my Japanese language abilities, the teacher said that we should listen to the Dharma with our feet. I thought to myself, "Here we go again, back to step one. He couldn't have said *ears*." I raised my hand to ask the teacher to clarify what he had said.

Once again the teacher said, "Listen to the Dharma with your feet." I had to ask him, "Did you say feet?"

He laughed and said, "Yes, feet. To listen to the Dharma means to listen with your entire being, from your head to your feet." He then gave an example of how Rennyo Shonin had worn out many, many pairs of sandals going from place to place listening to the Dharma.

If listening to the Dharma is an experience of our entire being, it is not something that we do by merely hearing the words from someone else. I believe that just as we may taste and sometimes even smell with senses other than our tongue and nose, we can listen as we sit. An example of this is with a lemon. Imagine a bright, perfectly shaped yellow lemon. Picture the shiny peel with the citrus oil glinting from it. Imagine this bright, firm lemon, the essence of which comes off onto your hand just by touching it. Then imagine cutting this lemon, feeling the juices splash a little onto your fingers and sting the small scratches on your hand. From this image, take one half of the cut lemon and bite into it.

As I write this description, I can feel the saliva ooze in my mouth and a small ache in my jaw from the tart taste of the lemon. I have just tasted a lemon with my mind. If we can taste with our mind, what do we mean by listening to the Dharma?

Within the *Kyogyoshinsho* there is a section that seems to say sitting meditation is not necessary. It is a passage that someone may use to say Shinran doesn't approve of sitting meditation:

Hymns according to the *Sutra of the Life of the Buddha* by Fa-chao:

What is to be called the right dharma?
What accords with truth is the true essence of the teaching.
Now is the time to determine and select right from wrong;
Test each particular one by one and allow no indistinctness.

The right dharma surpasses all things of the world!

Observance of precepts and seated meditation are called the right
    dharma,
But attainment of Buddhahood through the nembutsu is the true
    essence of the teaching.
Doctrines that do not accept the Buddha's words are nonbuddhist
    ways;
Views that reject the law of cause and effect are nihilistic.

The right dharma surpasses all things of the world!

> How can precepts and meditation be the right dharma?
> Nembutsu-samadhi is the true essence of the teaching.
> To see reality and awaken to mind, this is Buddha;
> How would Nembutsu-samadhi not accord with truth?
>
> *Kyogyoshinsho,* Chapter on Practice, *CWS*, Vol. 1, p. 40

The first lines of this hymn say, "What accords with truth is the true essence of the teaching. Now is the time to determine and select right from wrong; test each particular one by one and allow no indistinctness." I believe that if we are to find and decide the true essence, we must personally test a variety of practices for our own satisfaction.

Sitting meditation is a wonderful way to calm our very busy minds. Within our present society, many things happen in short sound bites. We rush to learn faster, play faster, read faster. The faster the computer the better, etc., etc. Many of us never take the time to slow down and observe our actions. We take things in without any reflection. In this manner, many things we think we hear are just merely noise. How can we listen to the Dharma with this type of mindset? It is also a way for us to follow the Nembutsu, or as this passage says, "Nembutsu Samadhi." Is using the Nembutsu while sitting any less effective than using the recite-respond-recite-respond type of Nembutsu we use in most of our BCA temples?

In another passage in the *Kyogyoshinsho*, Shinran states, "There are two kinds of shinjin (faith mind): one arises from hearing and the other from thought (reflection): This person's shinjin has arisen from hearing, but not from thought. Therefore, it is called 'imperfect realization of shinjin.'" Hearing the Dharma requires reflection upon our part. One of the sutras refers to Shakyamuni talking with members of the Kalama clan, explaining how to decide between right or wrong, like what we are doing in discussing meditation practices in BCA. I believe we should follow the Buddha's suggestion in this matter from Shakyamuni's talk to the Kalama clan.

Sitting on one side, the Kalamas, who were inhabitants of Kesaputta, said to the Blessed One: "There are some monks and Brahmins, venerable sir, who visit Kesaputta. They expound and explain only their own doctrines; the doctrines of others they despise, revile, and pull to pieces. Some other monks and Brahmins, too, venerable sir, come to Kesaputta. They also expound and explain only their own doctrines; the doctrines of others they despise, revile, and pull to pieces. Venerable sir, there is doubt, there is uncertainty in us concerning them. Which of these revered monks and Brahmins spoke the truth, and which falsehood?"

"It is proper for you, Kalamas, to doubt, to be uncertain; uncertainty has arisen in you about what is doubtful. Come, Kalamas. Do not go upon what has been acquired by repeated hearing; nor upon tradition; nor upon rumor; nor upon what is in a scripture; nor upon surmise; nor upon an axiom; nor upon specious reasoning; nor upon a bias towards a notion that has been pondered over; nor upon another's seeming ability; nor upon the consideration 'The monk is our teacher.' Kalamas, when you yourselves know: 'These things are bad; these things are blamable; these things are censured by the wise; undertaken and observed, these things lead to harm and ill,' abandon them."

We are in a time of transition within our Jodo Shinshu temples in the United States. If Jodo Shinshu is to become a vital part of the spiritual life of us denizens of the 21st century, we must be willing to evolve. Sitting meditation may not have been a part of our traditional service. Tradition is defined as "handing down beliefs and customs by word of mouth or by example without written instruction." We should try out a number of methodologies that can benefit our listening to the Dharma. Maybe sitting meditation will become a new tradition of our Salt Lake Buddhist Temple or maybe we will reject it. I believe that we should at least try it. I hope that some of you will be interested in taking part in beginning this possible new tradition at our temple.

I will close with Shakyamuni Buddha's advice on when one should accept a teaching: "Kalamas, when you yourselves know: 'These things are good; these things are not blamable; these things are praised by the wise; undertaken and observed, these things lead to benefit and happiness,' enter on and abide in them."

Sitting Namo Amida Butsu

◆◆◆

Rivers of blind passions, on entering the ocean—
The great compassionate Vow
Of unhindered light filling the ten quarters—
Become one in taste with that sea of wisdom.
"Koso Wasan" 42, *CWS*, p. 371

The question "What is Namo Amida Butsu?" can be very difficult to answer. Yet it is so simple to just say "Namo Amida Butsu." When I say Namo Amida Butsu, what is it that I am doing? It seems to change with the occasion. When I was a child, I would listen to the sensei tell us, "Please join me in Gassho." I would put my hands together and when he said, "Namo Amida Butsu," I would repeat, "Namo Amida Butsu." This would happen three times.

Later in my life, as I was riding on a plane hoping that I would be able to see my mother before she died, I imagined her in her bed dying, and suddenly "Namo Amida Butsu" came from my mouth. Sometimes when I am just breathing in and out, I can hear "Namo Amida Butsu." I have to admit that once in a while I will throw in a "Namo Amida Butsu" for luck. So what is this Namo Amida Butsu?

Is the Nembutsu that we call Namo Amida Butsu something that I am doing, or is it something that is around me that comes through me? The air I breathe is all around me, but it becomes a part of me when I breathe in and out. Breathing is said to be an involuntary physical act, meaning that whether or not we try, we just breathe. However, I am hooked up to a CPAP machine at night because the doctor says that sometimes I stop breathing in my sleep. So is it I who am breathing, or is it the machine?

In a similar vein, is it I who am saying Namo Amida Butsu, or is it Namo Amida Butsu that is coming through me? It is hard to say which is the cause and which the effect. In other words, is shinjin the result of Nembutsu or is Nembutsu the result of shinjin? What came first: the chicken or the egg?

Within Shinran's *Mattosho (Lamp for the Latter Ages)*, he states in reference to the saying of the Nembutsu as an act separate from shinjin:

> The reason is that the practice of Nembutsu is saying it perhaps once, perhaps ten times, on hearing and realizing that birth into the Pure Land is attained by saying the Name fulfilled in the Primal Vow. To hear this Vow and be completely without doubt is the one moment of shinjin. Thus, although shinjin and Nembutsu are two, since shinjin is to hear and not doubt that you are saved by only a single pronouncing, which is the fulfillment of practice, there is no shinjin separate from Nembutsu.

No matter what the cause or reason in Jodo Shinshu may be, it is often said to just say "Namo Amida Butsu." If you are unsure of how or why, just do it.

I believe the same can be said for the sitting meditation of Soto Zen. There are some who do not want to take part in meditation. They say that meditation is a self-powered practice while Jodo Shinshu teaches the other power of the Nembutsu. I do not believe meditation or Nembutsu is a practice per se. It is not the means to attain enlightenment. Rather it is a way to express that which has already been awakened to.

Within the Soto Zen School founded by Dogen Zenji, the type of meditation they do is called *shikantaza* which is usually translated as "just sitting." Dogen states in his *Fukanzazengi (Universally Recommended Practices for Zazen)*: "The zazen I speak of is not meditation practice [in the traditional Buddhist sense]. It is simply the dharma gate of peace and bliss, the practice-realization of totally culminated awakening." In my mind, there is no difference between this type of sitting and our saying the Nembutsu. This "practice-realization of totally culminated awakening" is shinjin.

To recite the Nembutsu as a response or with a deep sense of gratitude that comes from something more than myself is my Nembutsu practice. We may say this Nembutsu comes from the mind of Amida to my mind. In a similar manner, when I sit, it is an expression of the awakening of the mind of Amida within me. To sit or to say Namo Amida Butsu, I believe, are the same. As I sit, I breathe in and out. As I recite Namo Amida Butsu, it is as my breath. Both are the manifestation of the Great Compassion that embraces us all. I sit in Namo Amida Butsu.

Magic vs. Miso

◆ ◆ ◆

The Venerable Ananda tells the Buddha, "The Dharma friends (Kalyanamitra) are half the holy life." The Buddha responded, "Having good Dharma friends is the holy life. When a person has admirable people as friends, companions and comrades, they can be expected to develop and pursue the noble eightfold path."

Upaddha Sutra

I would like to tell you a story about a test of magic, miracles and simple faith. This is a story I first heard from the late Rev. Chijun Yakumo while he was the minister of the Salt Lake Buddhist Temple. This story is about a test for Buddhist priests, which happened long ago in the village of Yoshida in Hiroshima, Japan.

Many years ago, near the foot of the Chugoku Mountain Range, in the tiny village of Yoshida, a great test took place. For the citizens of Yoshida, the outcome of this test has had repercussions up until this very day. This test took place between two Buddhist priests, one from the Shingon sect of Buddhism and the other a Jodo Shinshu priest.

The Shingon priest was a remarkable man. He had trained himself in various mystical practices and was endowed with superhuman powers. He lived a very austere lifestyle. He would wake each morning before dawn to begin the various religious rituals from which he derived his immense powers. This man would eat only once a day and never after noon. Many of the villagers had claimed to witness miracles as a result of this very powerful master.

In comparison, the Jodo Shinshu priest was quite an ordinary individual. He loved to talk with the people of the village. He usually awoke around 6:00 a.m. for the morning service at his temple. He ate almost anything. He often amazed the townsfolk with how much he could eat. His favorite meal was *okonomiyaki* (a Japanese pizza) with a side order of miso soup over a big bowl of rice. As he went about town, you could often hear the villagers complaining, "There's nothing special about him. He's no different from us."

Both of these priests and their temples were very different from one another. However, the townspeople of this village would soon have to decide which priest and temple they preferred. It is common for temples in Japan to have only a few members. The town of Yoshida had only 60 families and two temples. Therefore, it was decided to select one of these two temples to remain as the village temple. The villagers then held a town meeting to decide what to do about this very difficult situation.

How could they decide which priest to keep? There were some villagers who thought an election of some sort should be held. Others felt that they should keep both temples and do what they could for both priests. There were many opinions but no obvious solutions. So they asked the elders of the village to decide on an appropriate way to decide which temple would remain. The elders came up with quite an interesting solution. It would be a test between the two priests.

The villagers would erect a large metal tub in the middle of the town square and fill it with water. Beneath this tub they would light a large fire to boil the water. Once the water was boiling, they would have the priests get into the boiling water, one at a time. The villagers would watch how each of the priests reacted and completed this test. Observing the results, they would determine which priest would remain in the village.

On the appointed day, both priests were called to the town square and informed of the difficult situation the village was in. Each priest agreed to take part in this unusual test. The Shingon priest was a very powerful Tantric master, trained in esoteric forms of meditation and ritual. The Jodo Shinshu priest was a kind and gentle man, without any special powers. As one could have expected, the powerful Tantric master volunteered to go first. The Jodo Shinshu priest let out a sigh of relief and thanked the priest for volunteering.

Before he entered the water, the Shingon priest performed a ritual of purification and recited a number of sutras. Following this, he sat down in meditation with both hands together in gassho. There was complete silence throughout the village as they all stood mesmerized by this master of Esoteric Buddhism. The villagers and the Jodo Shinshu priest watched breathlessly as the priest stood and leapt into the scalding water, landing in the middle of the cauldron.

Although the fire had died down, the water was still bubbling around him; yet this priest's magic protected him from feeling any pain. He sat down in this water and continued his chanting of the sutras. He remained in the water for a full ten minutes, not even breaking into a sweat. He then got up, bowed to the villagers and leapt back out of the cauldron. The villagers and the Jodo Shinshu priest broke into thundering applause. No one there had ever witnessed such an amazing feat of self-control and power. It was now the Jodo Shinshu priest's turn.

The Jodo Shinshu priest thought to himself, "Maybe it's only an illusion and the water isn't really that hot." He placed his finger in the water to check and immediately pulled it out. The water was no longer bubbling, but it was still extremely hot. Thinking, "This water is hotter than the miso soup I ate this morning," he had an idea. "Ladies and gentlemen, I have a favor to ask each of you before I begin my test. I would like each of you to return home and bring back your bathtubs." The villagers thought it was a strange request, but realizing that the results of this test would determine the future of Buddhism in their village, they agreed. While the villagers were away the Jodo Shinshu priest took some of the water and made miso soup and placed a few bottles of sake into the hot water.

When the villagers returned he announced, "The water in this tub is now perfect for taking a bath. It would be such a waste for only me to enjoy this bath and water. That is why I asked each of you to go and get your own tubs, so that we may enjoy a comforting bath under this beautiful blue sky, enjoying this miso and sake that I have readied." The townspeople all agreed that indeed it was a beautiful day for an outdoor bath and they joined the priest in their tubs as he stepped into the larger one.

As the priest and villagers finished the sake and ended their baths, so ended the test for the priests. Now the villagers had to decide which priest and temple should remain in their village. It was obvious to everyone there that the Shingon priest was a remarkable, almost superhuman individual, and many of the villagers thought he should remain. However, the wisest elder of the village spoke out: "I, too, agree that the Shingon priest with his magic is very impressive. The Jodo Shinshu priest doesn't have any magical powers. He eats miso in the morning just like the rest of us. However, if we were to pick the Shingon priest with his power, Buddhism teaches us that no man can escape death, so what will become of our village if this powerful master dies? What will become of his temple and all of us?"

All the villagers nodded their heads in agreement. He continued, "As I have said, the Shingon priest is a remarkable man and the Jodo Shinshu priest is average at best. However, as a result of his ordinary life, his understanding of the Dharma is at a level most of us can understand, and if he were to die, we could easily find another priest to replace him. Therefore, I believe we should allow the Jodo Shinshu priest to remain." There was no one that could argue with this man's logic. It was a case of magic vs. miso, with the miso winning. To this very day in the village of Yoshida there is a Jodo Shinshu temple.

This story has two lessons for us to contemplate. The first has to do with the selection of the priest. Within our BCA temples, I have often heard members complaining about their ministers: Why doesn't our minister have the type of program that minister does? Our minister's

English is terrible and I can't understand anything he says. He doesn't do this or that, ad nauseam. There have been good and bad priests since religion began to have priests. There have been many religions that have failed even with amazing priests. However, maybe the reason Jodo Shinshu has done so well and lasted for hundreds of years is the quality of its priests.

Jodo Shinshu is not a clergy-centered religion and actually considers gurus heretical. The Jodo Shinshu priest should be considered a Dharma friend (*kalyanamitra*–Sanskrit, *zenchishiki*–Japanese) rather than a guru. The emphasis within Jodo Shinshu is on the teachings and faith of the membership. Therefore, if the priest is bad, the members must rely upon their own initiative and belief to keep the temple going. With the shortage of ministers within BCA, the temples will have to rely more and more upon their members. Now is the time to realize this, since there are still ministers upon whom to depend and ask questions. The next time you feel like complaining about the minister and his or her lack of ability, remember this test of magic versus miso and the power of miso and everyday life.

The second lesson, or rather a metaphor, for this story concerns the power of the Nembutsu. If you look at the boiling water as the Dharma (Buddhist Teaching), you can see how within some sects of Buddhism only the priest is allowed to touch upon it. It is only the priests who are allowed to bask and understand the nature of this profound truth. It is from deep self-purification and sometimes a little magic that one is allowed to become one with this awesome power. However, with the Nembutsu teachings, the power of the Dharma is to be shared by all. The priest powered by a little miso and sake, explains and speaks about the Dharma through his own life experience. His role is that of a Dharma friend. Everyone can see and experience the benefits of the Dharma and enjoy the warm embrace as one unified Sangha.

Old Age

Old age is the second of the Four Noble Truths and may be my favorite, since it means I'm still alive. This section contains some of the stories that I have learned from being alive, aging in both mind and body. It also shows how through life we have the opportunity to learn from the entire world, not just the small cultural arena we have been born into. I have learned a great deal from friends of mine who were not Buddhist. It's always good to get a second opinion.

I Put My Face in Buddha

◆ ◆ ◆

A person once expressed exactly what was on his mind in the following manner, "My heart is just like a basket into which you pour water. While I am there in the room where the Buddha-Dharma is taught, I feel the gratefulness and the sacredness of the Teachings. However, once I leave, my heart reverts to what it had been with nothing retained." Shonin Rennyo replied, "Immerse the basket in the water. We should leave ourselves immersed in the Dharma. All the wrongs that we do are based on the fact that we have not received Shinjin. What all zenchishikis teach as 'bad' is our habitual thinking that being without Shinjin is the constant and the normal thing." Thus spoke the Shonin.

Rennyo Shonin, *Goichidai Kikigaki*

It was a warm Sunday morning. The room was very quiet, with the incense wafting throughout the hondo. As usual, the adults were sitting in the back, with the Sunday school classes in the front pews. As everyone stood for the gatha, "In Lumbini's Garden," Mikey reached into his back pocket and pulled something out. Mouthing the words to the gatha and trying not to move his upper body, Mikey passed his new set of baseball cards to Jerry. Reaching over, Jerry took them from Mikey's hand and began scanning through the set.

After the gatha, after everyone had sat back down, Jerry whispered to Mikey, "Wow, where did you get all these cards? I'll trade you my Roger Maris for your Mickey Mantle." Suddenly, out of the incense-filled air came a large hand. Grabbing Jerry by the back of his shirt, the hand pulled his head back and up, towards a looming set of lips.

"SHHHH!!! Be quiet and put those cards away before I take them from you. Sensei is about to talk. You kids had better listen."

41

Sheepishly, Jerry handed the cards back to Mikey. Holding back a giggle, Mikey took them and put them back in his pocket. Squirming in his seat, Jerry mumbled to himself, "Jeez, I can't understand what he's saying anyway."

"I heard that! Just sit there and something ought to sink in. Show some respect for Sensei and the other people who want to listen."

"All right, all right I get it," said Jerry. Mumbling, he added, "Don't get your panties in a knot over it" …mumble, mumble….

"What did you *say?*" said the Dharma school teacher menacingly.

"Nothin'," said Jerry. The other kids in the class giggled. Sensei came up to the podium with a big smile on his face, "Ohayo Gozaimasu! Pleezu put your hanzu togeza and repeato afta me. I putu my feisu in Buddha."

"I put my face in Buddha," responded the Sangha.

"I putu my feisu in Dharma," recited Sensei.

"I put my face in Dharma," responded the Sangha.

"I putu my feisu in Sangha," recited Sensei.

"I putu my feisu in Sangha, sankyu beddy muchi." Bowing and giggling, Jerry tried to imitate Sensei's broken English. The rest of his class burst out laughing. Wham! Jerry felt himself lifted out of his seat and hurriedly rushed out into the lobby for a stern lecture about the importance of the proper etiquette when attending Sunday school services. Jerry wondered, "Well, I guess I won't get to hear Sensei's message after all. Will it still sink in?"

Thus began another Sunday school service some 30 years ago. I can still hear my parents' lecture at home. Although my sister may have forgotten what Sensei had actually said, she definitely remembered to tell my parents about my getting pulled out of the service. "What's wrong with you? You embarrass the entire family by acting that way. What you do reflects upon *Bachan* (Grandma), *Jichan* (Grandpa), the both of us, your sister, Auntie Maxine, your cousins—everyone in the family. Sensei is trying very hard to teach you kids. I know it might be hard to listen, but if you try hard enough, something will definitely sink in."

Well, some 30 years have passed since I heard similar lectures all through my youth. Surprisingly, something must have sunk in. For now it is my turn to watch the Dharma school students squirm, with the parents and adults sitting in the back rows and the teachers keeping an eye on the more restless students. I'm now the one saying, "Good morning everyone!" All the years of squirming around, trying to get something to sink in, must have done something. For I am now the minister, struggling to find something appropriate to talk about during our weekly Dharma school service.

It's not always easy coming up with something new and relevant. I talk to the other ministers about what they have used during their Dharma school *howa* (talk). Working with the Dharma school students is one of the most rewarding parts of being a minister. However, it can also be one of the most difficult. I can imagine the difficulty the senseis I grew up with had in trying to come up with a relevant message in a foreign language, week after week.

This year has been my tenth year as a minister of the BCA. I also turned 40 years old and now have a daughter sitting in the Dharma school services. Over these ten years as a minister and 30 years before as a Dharma school student, teacher, YBA member, etc., I have attended countless temple meetings—local, district and national. I have also attended a great variety of conferences—from local and district conferences to national and world conferences. What I have learned from all of this can be summed up in the "Three Treasures" that the sensei spoke about so long ago. "I put my face in Buddha. I put my face in Dharma. I put my face in Sangha."

Although Sensei may have had some difficulty with English, I still remember his message. We all know that Sensei was trying to say "faith," and now the Dharma school service books have a variety of readings, such as "I take refuge in." Although it was years before I realized the word Sensei was saying was "faith" rather than "face," I now like the idea of putting my face into the Three Treasures.

I have watched my daughter learn to walk. When I call her to me or when she greets me as I come home, she runs towards me full force, her face slamming into me. It is with her entire being that she comes to me, embracing me as I embrace her in my arms. In a similar manner, it is with our entire being that we should immerse ourselves in the

Dharma, to be embraced. As Rennyo stated in the passage I began this essay with, "We should leave ourselves immersed in the Dharma."

Over the years, I have also noticed that there were others like my former Dharma school teacher. Although their original intentions may be good, they often distract the individual and themselves from immersing themselves in the Three Treasures. Everyone who attends temple meetings and conferences knows the people I am referring to. These are the individuals that love to stand up and complain about details, protocol, etc. We hear them in many forms: "The sensei must speak better English, or the BCA should do this or that"; "The temple should be more business-like," etc. Although their original intentions may be good, their self-righteous attitudes are obvious and they often keep us from getting on with the important matters at hand. Our temples have survived for many, many years. It is the Dharma that holds it all together. Everyone wants the temples and BCA to be better, but let's not lose sight of the original intent. Let's put our face, our entire being in the Buddha, Dharma and Sangha. Keep this attitude fundamental.

My parents would scold me for messing around in Sunday school (way back then, it wasn't called Dharma school). Even while being scolded, I realized the deep regard with which they held the Three Treasures. They understood that it may have been difficult for me to understand all of what Sensei said. However, I never heard them say anything bad about the ministers. On the contrary, the ministers were always held in high regard. I know that ministers make mistakes; I can tell you many of my own. However, my family's regard for the ministers and the temple helped to shape my own feelings toward the Dharma. Being pulled out of the service did nothing other than pull me away from Sensei's lesson and possibly distract others.

Those who always complain should look at what their attitude is doing to themselves and their own families. Is it bringing them to the original intent of the Nembutsu teachings? Is it causing them to merely become frustrated and pull further away from the Buddha, Dharma and Sangha? As I told my Dharma school teacher way back when, I must say to you now, "Don't get your shorts or panties (whatever the case may be) in a knot." Let's all allow ourselves to become immersed in this wonderful Nembutsu teaching. Do not distract others with your own personal demons. However, that subject is for another lesson. Running, stumbling, leaping, I put my face in Buddha, Dharma and Sangha. Namo Amida Butsu.

Dancing in the Twilight Zone

◆◆◆

The Nembutsu is not a mantra that beings recite to the Buddha, it is the Buddha's invitation to beings to accept the liberation that he has already obtained for them....When this realization is experienced, it comes as a moment of ecstatic, bodily, dancing joy. Nothing needs to be done! Everything is right as it is! "Namu Amida Butsu!" we shout in gratitude.

Roger J. Corless, *The Vision of Buddhism: The Space Under the Tree*

It has been a rather hectic and unusual month because of my knee surgery. I would like to thank the various organizations and people who sent me gifts and get well cards. Thanks to our temple member, Dr. Brian Fukushima, my knee surgery went well and with rehab it should be as good as can be expected for a fifty-one-year-old knee. Before my accident, I thought I understood what it meant to be disabled or handicapped, but it is nothing like the reality. The whole experience has given me a perspective on another way of life and living. It has truly been a humbling experience for which I am profoundly grateful.

It has also been a rather strange month, reminding me of one of those old *The Twilight Zone* episodes, where at the beginning we hear Rod Serling's introduction: "You're traveling through another dimension. A dimension not only of sight and sound, but of mind. A journey

45

into a wondrous land whose boundaries are that of imagination. Ladies and gentlemen, this evening's episode concerns a man waiting to begin a trip to California, but without knowing it, he has taken a detour into the Twilight Zone."

The episode begins with my daughter Taylor coming to see me before I left for California. With my leg in a brace, I couldn't drive to pick her up from school as usual; I didn't think I would see her before I left for California. As I waited at home, feeling somewhat sorry for myself about not getting to see her, I heard the back patio door open. I thought it was strange and that maybe somehow Ponzu, my dog, had opened it and gotten out. Then I heard Taylor's voice, "Hi, Dad! How you doing?"

I asked her how she had gotten to the house. She said that she had been playing at a friend's house after school, and when the friend's father was going to drive her home, she asked if he would bring her to my house. She said she knew she wouldn't get to see me for a whole week and wanted to try to see me before I left. As with all dramatic episodes on television, there's a plot twist for Taylor and me. It was that she had forgotten to tell her mom that she was coming to my house. Her mom had been calling around to find her and didn't know where she had gone. She was very upset when Taylor called and told her she was at my house. Taylor knew she was in trouble; I tried to tell her it was my fault, since my not being able to drive messed up our regular schedule. She said, "No, Dad, I was wrong for not letting Mom know what I was doing. But I'm really glad I got to see you before you left."

I was so happy she made the extra effort to visit me, but even prouder that she faced the responsibility of making a mistake and was willing to face the consequences herself without making excuses or having them made for her. It was the beginning of a series of life lessons. This incident taught me how my daughter loves me as much as I love her and that she is growing up with personal integrity. What more could a father ask for?

(**Commercial Break**)

We then went to the airport, which was another adventure: going through security in a wheelchair. I fretted on the plane, worrying about how I was going to get around the next week with just a walker. As I was pushed to baggage claim in Orange County, Rev. Marvin Harada was waiting for me with a wheelchair. I was a little hungry, and Rev. Harada had also brought me a Vietnamese sandwich (my favorite) to eat, since he thought I may not have eaten dinner.

The next morning I didn't have anything to do except sit in my hotel room. I had signed up earlier to play in the BCA ministers' golf tournament that morning; however, because of my knee, I couldn't. It was cheaper to fly in as scheduled rather than to change my flight to a later date. My friend Wendell Hamamoto took the afternoon off to take me to a nearby Indian casino. I didn't win money in the casino. That would have been too abnormal. However, throughout the week I could almost hear the tinkling of Glinda the Good Witch's magic wand granting my wishes. I had friends like Revs. Harada, Matsumoto, Shinseki, and Okamoto pushing me around in the wheelchair before, after and during the meetings, and between meetings they would check to see if I needed anything like coffee or meeting handouts. It was really a humbling experience to have such wonderful friends.

(Commercial Break)

It was now Thursday morning. I could relax a bit. Carmela was flying in for the IBS symposium on Buddhism and music. If Carmela is around, I know that things will work out. For example, the week before, when our past temple president Kay Terashima passed away, I was so worried about how I would get things done for the funeral preparation. I was still taking quite a bit of pain medication and my thinking was blurry. I couldn't think and I couldn't drive. Carmela came charging in on a white horse and had her secretary reschedule all her patients for the afternoon of the Makuragyo, for the viewing and for the day of the funeral. When she is around, it is as though I have an extra set of hands and feet and a better brain. As a result of her being there, the meeting seemed to flow by.

The IBS symposium was a series of lectures on the topic "What is Buddhist Music?" It seemed a custom fit for our temple's recent participation in the Interfaith Roundtable Concert at the Mormon Tabernacle. I was beginning to get used to everything going my way—

maybe too much so—and beginning to take all this kindness for granted, when the conference banquet began.

Carmela wheeled me into the banquet and things seemed to be okay, but as the dinner wore on, I realized I was trapped in my place. If I wanted to leave, it would require a lot of people to move their chairs so I could be pushed out. I sat trapped for almost three hours, and that was without an official banquet speaker. When we finally got out, we went to our room. I had been looking forward to listening to the band playing at the dance scheduled after the banquet. Instead of a speaker, Rev. Harada had arranged for a dance featuring a band that played songs from our YBA days. When I first heard about the dance, I wasn't really enthusiastic. I'm not a dancer, and when Carmela asks me to dance with her, it is not a pretty sight. However, I was now in a wheelchair and had a great excuse for not dancing. I could just listen to the band. When we got to the room, Carmela was rather tired and wasn't sure if she wanted to go to the dance. This should have been a sign for me that I was entering into the Twilight Zone.

(Final Commercial Break)

Our room was on the fourth floor of the hotel, but we could clearly hear the music playing. It was almost as though we were being called to the dance. They were playing songs that I really liked: really old-school-type music such as Earth, Wind and Fire, The Stylistics, The Whispers, etc. Carmela even commented on how well we could hear the music from our room. It was the type of music I heard when I went to my first Western Young Buddhist League (WYBL) Conference.

Our memories are such that we have a tendency to filter out most of the unpleasant things and look to the past with rose-colored glasses. It was the same with my memories of those WYBL conferences. They did change my way of thinking and really helped me define and decide who and what I wanted to be in life. I was 16 years old when I first attended a conference. At that conference I saw close to 900 other young Japanese American Buddhists. It was a cultural shock. It was probably one of the first things that really influenced my becoming a Buddhist priest. It also helped that at the conference were hundreds of cute Japanese American girls around my age. I wanted to go back to that

48

dance and relive some of that experience.

Carmela pushed me towards the music, down the elevator, through the hotel. I began to see groups of middle-aged people dressed in dark-colored clothes. As we got closer to the music and passed by clumps of people, I noticed they would kind of look the two of us up and down. It was *exactly* like those old YBA dances. They were checking us out, who we were, what we were wearing, etc., etc. They were the same people from those earlier dances, over thirty years ago, but they were OLD! There was a table with people checking our tickets to see if we belonged. Suddenly, I felt the insecurity of a teenager hoping to fit in.

Inside the pavilion it was very dark. There were some couples dancing, but many more were just sitting around tables or standing there checking us out. As we walked inside, I noticed that none of my friends were there; we didn't know anyone. Carmela would guide us through the crowds of people, but it was extremely claustrophobic. I saw a minister and his wife go out on the dance floor. However, I didn't think of him as a colleague. I thought to myself, "That's cute, the sensei is going out, trying to fit in. He wants to act young." And then the realization hit me: if he is old and everyone else in the room is old, then I'm old too! I asked Carmela if she would mind leaving early. She felt uncomfortable also, so we left.

We went up to the conference hospitality room. Coming through the door, someone said, "Hi, Hirano Sensei." I felt a warm wave wash over me. Dot Richeda and Reiko Watanabe from Salt Lake and James Aoki and Steve Kato from Ogden were eating and drinking in the room. I felt like Dorothy waking up in the *Wizard of Oz* and seeing Auntie Em's face. One of the other ministers who grew up in BCA and had also gone to those early WYBL dances asked me, "Did you go to the dance?" I said, "We did, but it felt really strange." He replied, "Yeah, it was like being in the Twilight Zone—everything was the same, but inside the clothes were old people!"

Everything came into perspective. He was exactly right: we were old and I was so happy to be my age, to be where I was. It was just as Dorothy said: "There's no place like home." I had once been a young man searching for my identity. It was a painful journey at times, but all along the way, because of many good friends of the Dharma (*zench-ishiki*), I was just where I was supposed to be. I am okay just as I am, embraced in the wondrous compassion of Amida Buddha.

As the camera pans off into a star-filled sky and *The Twilight Zone* theme starts, I can be seen dancing with joy, saying "Namo Amida Butsu!" Rod Serling's voice fills the room saying, "The Nembutsu is not a mantra that beings recite to the Buddha, it is the Buddha's invitation to beings to accept the liberation that he has already obtained for them.... When this realization is experienced, it comes as a moment of ecstatic, bodily, dancing joy. Nothing needs to be done! Everything is right as it is! 'Namo Amida Butsu!' we shout in gratitude. This is a very important lesson our friend has just learned, dancing in The Twilight Zone."

Santa's Golden Chain

I am a link in Amida's golden chain of love that stretches
  around the world.
I will keep my link bright and strong.
I will be kind and gentle to every living thing and protect
  all who are weaker than myself.
I will think pure and beautiful thoughts, say pure and
  beautiful words and do pure and beautiful deeds.
May every link in Amida's golden chain of love be bright
  and strong, and may we all attain perfect peace.

Dharma school service book

Taylor ran home from school hurt and confused. Hurling open the front door, he ran straight to his room, not saying anything to his mom or sister. As he lay on top of his bed, he thought to himself, "Could it be *true*? Santa won't be coming to my house this year?"

Earlier in the day, Ms. Tuttle, his first grade teacher, had asked the students to stand up and tell the class what they would be doing over their holiday vacation. When it was his turn, Taylor proudly stood up and explained to the class what his family would be doing.

"First of all, on Christmas Eve we go to the Koyo, my favorite Japanese restaurant and have dinner with my family. My cousins and I see who can eat the most gyoza and shrimp tempura."

"Taylor, could you explain to the class what gyoza and shrimp tempura are?" asked Ms. Tuttle.

Taylor made a sheepish face at his teacher and explained, "Gyoza is like a little fried Japanese burrito and shrimp tempura is shrimp with bread stuff on the outside."

"Thank you, Taylor. Please continue."

"After we finish dinner, we go to my auntie's house for dessert. My cousins and I get to open up a few presents. After we get home, I put on my new pajamas. Every year my sister and I get new pajamas. It's in the present Mom always makes us open up on Christmas Eve. I always have a hard time falling asleep on Christmas Eve, but my mom says the new pajamas help.

"On Christmas morning my sister and I run to wake our parents up. But before we can open our presents, my dad makes us go to our *obutsudan* and say thank you to Buddha."

"Excuse me again, Taylor, but what is an obutsudan?"

"The obutsudan is our little Buddhist altar we have at home. Jeez, Ms. Tuttle, you sure ask a lot of questions. Didn't you go to college?"

"Sorry, Taylor. Yes, I went to college, but some of the things you are explaining are a little different from what some of us are accustomed to."

"Really? I thought everyone did the same thing?"

"No, Taylor, we all have different ways of celebrating the holidays, that's why I wanted you all to tell us what you do."

"Oh. I get it. Well, when we stand in front of the obutsudan, we say thank you Buddha by saying, 'Namo Amida Butsu.' That's how we say it in Buddha language. My dad says that Santa is always checking to see if we are grateful for what we have. If we aren't grateful, he might take the presents back. So, after we do that, we get to open up our presents. In the evening we go to my other auntie's house for Christmas dinner."

"Thank you, Taylor. Who will be next?"

"Wait Ms. Tuttle. There's more!"

"Excuse me, Taylor. Please continue."

"Between Christmas and New Year's Day we go to the temple and make mochi."

"Taylor, what is uhh…mochi?"

Taylor looked at his teacher with a surprised look. "You don't know what mochi is either?"

"I'm afraid I don't, Taylor, and probably many of the other students don't know either."

"Well, mochi is smashed rice that we pound with a big wooden hammer in a stone bowl until it gets soft and squishy."

"Ughh!" said some of the kids in class.

"We then make it into little flat balls. Some of it we eat and some we pile onto a plate with two pieces of mochi stacked with a tangerine on top. We put that mochi in our obutsudan. My mom says that the mochi is to express thanks to the Buddha and it expresses my dad's and her wish that my sister and I stay strong and healthy. After we make mochi we have a New Year's Eve service at the temple. After the service we ring the temple's bell 108 times."

"Taylor, why do you ring the temple bell?"

"I'm not really sure, but it has something to do with ringing out the old year, I think? Ms. Tuttle, I'm not sure why we do everything, ya know. You could probably ask my mom. I think she knows."

"Thank you, Taylor. I'll do that."

"Well, once everyone has rung the bell, we get together and eat noodles. When we wake up on New Year's morning, we go to the obutsudan like on Christmas and then we eat mochi soup."

"Yuck!" the students said. Taylor gave some of them a dirty look, but continued.

"We eat the soup and then go to the temple. After that we get money from my grandparents and all my aunts and uncles. It's called *Toshi* something, I'm not sure why we get it, but I'm glad I get it."

"Cool," said some of Taylor's classmates. Taylor smiled proudly.

"After going to the temple, we go to my other auntie's house and have a big feast, with all kinds of Japanese and American food. It's really cool."

"Is that it, Taylor?"

"Yup…and then we have to come back to school the next day."

"Well, thank you, Taylor. That certainly was informative for all of us." Taylor sat down feeling rather good about himself. At 2:45 the bell to go home rang. It was then that the trouble began.

In the hallway, as Taylor was putting his coat on to go home, Nathan and Jackson came up to him and said, "What's all that ooga booga Buddha stuff? Christmas is only for good Christians. Christmas is Jesus's birthday, not Buddha's."

"Yeah," said Jackson. "Mochi, pochi. It sounds like poop to me. You eat poop and say ooga booga Buddha. Santa doesn't like Buddha boys and poop eaters. Santa isn't going to come to a Buddha boy's house. He comes to our house because we believe in Jesus and it's his birthday."

Taylor could feel tears starting to well in his eyes. He didn't want anyone to see him cry. He was so mad that he just pushed Nathan and Jackson out of his way and ran out of the school. All the way home, all he could hear was "ooga booga Buddha, Santa isn't going to come to a Buddha boy's house."

All of these thoughts ran through his mind as he lay in his bed. There was a soft knock on his door. "Taylor? Can I come in? Is everything okay?" It was his mother.

"I don't feel too good, Mom." The door to his room opened and his mom came in with his sister Kacie tagging along. His mother sat down next to him and felt his forehead. "You do feel a little warm. I hope you aren't coming down with something." Kacie jumped on his bed. Kacie was Taylor's four-year-old sister. Kacie put her face right up to his. "Taylor's been crying, Taylor's been crying... ha ha ha ha ha ha," said Kacie.

"Kacie!" scolded their mother. "Taylor, is something wrong? Please tell me what's wrong." Taylor began to cry and his mom held him in her arms as he somehow managed to tell her the things that had happened at school.

"Oh, honey, I'm so sorry that you had to go through all that," his mother lovingly told him. "I know it can sometimes be difficult being Japanese and Buddhist and living here in America. When I was little, I would get teased at school too."

"Y...you ddid, Mmmom?" he managed to say.

"Yes, I did, and so did your father. It isn't always easy. But being Japanese and Buddhist is nothing to be ashamed of. Like we always tell you and Kacie, you should be very proud of being Japanese and Buddhist. Some people can be mean, but it's because they don't know any better. I'm really sorry that you had to go through this. But sometimes we have to go through hurtful things to really grow up. I'm really proud of you for saying what you did in school today."

"Y...you're p...proud of me?"

"Very proud, Taylor. You are a very special boy to be able to stand up in class and say those things." Taylor sat up in bed looking up into his mother's kind eyes.

"Really, Mom? But what about Santa and what Nathan and Jackson said about Santa not liking Buddha boys?"

"I don't think Santa would agree with them. I'd have to wonder what Santa would think about Nathan's and Jackson's behavior today. Taylor, when you think of Santa, tell me what you think of?"

"Well...he's a big, happy guy...who gives good boys and girls presents."

"Why does he give you those presents?"

"He wants all of us kids to be kind and gentle to one another. He watches what we're doing to make sure we're good in that way."

"That's right. Do you remember the Golden Chain that we say in

Dharma school?"

"Sure I do, Mom. Remember, I had to lead the Golden Chain two weeks ago?"

"I remember, Taylor. Would you say it for me now?"

"I am a link in Amida Buddha's Golden Chain of love that stretches around the world."

Kacie and his mom joined him as he continued. "I will keep my link bright and strong. I will be kind and gentle to every living thing and protect all who are weaker than myself. I will think pure and beautiful thoughts, say pure and beautiful words, and do pure and beautiful deeds. May every link in Amida's Golden Chain of love be bright and strong, and may we all attain perfect peace."

"Except Nathan and Jackson," said Taylor.

"Now, Taylor."

"I was just kidding, Mom. So you think Santa will still come to visit me?"

"Yes, honey, I'm sure Santa will be visiting you."

"But what about that stuff they said about Jesus?"

"Well, Taylor. I'm not an expert on Jesus since I'm Buddhist. But everything I've heard about Jesus seems to tell me that Jesus was trying to follow the Golden Chain in his life. What good Christians try to do is to follow his example. As Buddhists we are trying to be kind and gentle to every living thing, just as he was. Jesus had a thing called the Golden Rule. It goes, 'Do unto others as you would have them do unto you.' What that means is that you shouldn't do to other people what you wouldn't want them to do to you."

"That kind of sounds like the way Sensei explained the Golden Chain to us. Since we are all links in the Golden Chain, we shouldn't do anything bad to one another. Because what I do affects everyone else in the chain. Do you think Sensei is Christian?"

"No, Taylor, Sensei is definitely not Christian. But what Sensei, your father and I hope you learn and what the Christians hope their children learn is very similar in many respects. If that's the case, I don't see anything wrong with a Buddhist celebrating such a kind and smart man's birthday. Do you?"

"No, Mom. You're right. I think it's good for us to say 'Namo Amida Butsu' to Jesus for having such a good birthday. Is Nathan's and Jackson's religion just like mine?"

"No, Taylor. There are many things that are different. However, when it comes to what people often call the spirit of Christmas—"

"What's that, Mom?"

"The spirit of Christmas is the good feeling that comes over most people during this time of year. You know how when we visit the malls and you see the children laughing and smiling with their mommies and daddies—"

"That's a lot of fun, isn't it, Mom."

"It sure is, honey. This feeling goes beyond just our family and spreads out as a feeling of kindness and generosity to everyone. This lesson is similar in most religions. Although we are Buddhist, this Christmas spirit is the heart of Buddhism."

"You mean even though Nathan and Jackson may be mean, I should be kind and gentle back to them? That's kind of hard to do."

"Well, what do you think, Taylor? Would you want them to feel as bad as they made you feel?"

"No, Mom, I'll just Christmas spirit them back. Kind and gentle to every living thing, even Nathan and Jackson."

"You got it, kiddo. You amaze me. Now do you feel better?"

"I sure do, Mom. Thanks a lot."

"Well, you had better get ready for dinner. Tonight's Christmas Eve, so we have to hurry to Koyo as soon as Dad gets home."

That night, Taylor and his family had a wonderful Christmas Eve together. He and Kacie dressed in their new pajamas and snuggled down in their beds with visions of gyoza and shrimp tempura dancing in their heads. During the middle of the night Taylor was awakened from his slumber, and to his amazement, as he heard a ringing of bells, he also heard a bright, jolly voice proclaim, "Namo Amida Butsu, Merry Christmas to all and to all a good night!"

Since many of the traditions and words that Taylor has expressed in this story are not fully understood or recognized by many, I thought it would be helpful to have a short glossary as reference. It is important to understand it for yourself. However, unlike Taylor who does not know why the bell is rung 108 times on New Year's Eve, if your child or grandchild were to ask you, would you be able to explain the reason? It's nice to know the answers or to learn them together. Many of these traditions are slowly changing or being forgotten. I feel that it is important that we maintain some of them for the benefit of future generations to know who or what they are and where they come from.

I have used a variety of sources for this glossary. I will recommend some of them to you at the end.

Amida Buddha: Amida Buddha is the central Buddha within the Jodo Shinshu belief. Within the obutsudan Amida is the single Buddha embodied there. Amida Buddha is not a God or deity. Amida is the anthropomorphic representation of Ultimate Truth, Wisdom and Compassion. Amida is the Japanese reading of the original Sanskrit name combining two names, *Amitabha* (infinite light), and *Amitayus* (infinite life). This represents the unlimited aspect of this Truth, beyond time and space.

Butsudan: The obutsudan is a Buddhist altar used by Buddhist families in their homes. The character "o" that is placed before many of the words in this glossary is honorific. In Jodo Shinshu Buddhist families, the obutsudan can vary in size and shape, from a small scroll to an elaborate wooden box with varying degrees of ornamentation. Inside the obutsudan, the most common central image is of Amida Buddha or the six characters that say "Namo Amida Butsu." Some obutsudan contain drawers in which the family places important records, such as the names of deceased family members or the Buddhist names of the family.

Traditionally each family has an obutsudan placed in a central area of the home or special room. This signifies the central importance of the Buddhist teachings within the family's life. Daily offerings of rice or various items are placed inside or outside the altar. The family conducts daily rituals such as incense burning, sutra chanting or merely coming before the altar and placing their hands together in gassho and reciting the Nembutsu.

Dharma school: Dharma meaning "teaching of the Buddha." The name Dharma school was adopted by the Buddhist Churches of America to differentiate the Christian Sunday school from theirs. However, most Dharma schools are held on Sunday mornings.

Golden Chain: A short poem to teach children about the basic intent of the Buddha's teaching. It is recited at Dharma school services with children taking turns leading the others.

Gyoza: Small, crescent-shaped, pan-fried Japanese dumpling, usually filled with minced pork and vegetables.

Joya-e: This means "last night gathering." It is the year-end service held at the temple. At this service, it is a time for all the members to get together to reflect on the past year and express gratitude for the various causes and conditions, both good and bad, that have made it possible for them to live this one year.

Many temples will ring their temple bell 108 times. This is called *Joya-e no Kane,* "the bell of the last night." The number 108 symbolically represents the 108 passions or *bonno* which afflict us human beings. This ringing of the bell is a reminder of the 108 passions, which entangle us. The bell is rung as a reminder to try to go beyond our ego attachments in the coming year. However, if we are unable, we recognize that within the Nembutsu we are fine.

Kagami Mochi: Meaning "mirror *mochi,*" also called *kasane mochi,* "piled mochi." Since Heian times this has been served on all festive occasions. It is called *kagami mochi* because of the similarity of its shape to the traditional Japanese mirror. It is also called kasane mochi since the New Year's offering of mochi on the altar is made up of two cakes stacked one on top of the other.

On the top of this mound is placed a tangerine or orange. Traditionally the citrus fruit was a yellow-orange fruit called a *dai-dai.* This fruit would turn yellow-orange in the winter but turn green again if left on the tree until spring. This seeming return to youth came to represent the prosperity of children from age to age. The term "from age to age" is also pronounced *daidai* in Japanese.

Mochi: A rice cake made from glutinous rice. The steamed rice is pounded in a big wooden mortar with a wooden mallet until it takes on a sticky consistency. The soft mochi is then rolled into round cakes or is spread into a large square to be cut into smaller pieces. The making of mochi is called *mochitsuki*. Traditionally mochitsuki was done in many households during the holiday season. Now many Buddhist temples or Japanese social groups pound mochi before the holidays as a cultural and fund raising event. It is a custom to eat mochi on New Year's Day since it is regarded as a good omen.

Nembutsu or Nenbutsu: Literally means "Think Buddha." In Pure Land Buddhism, Nembutsu refers to saying Namo Amida Butsu, "I take refuge in Amida Buddha." This recitation is the wisdom and compassion of the Buddha being expressed in our everyday life. It is not a prayer, petition or mantra. It is our expression of gratitude for Amida Buddha's wisdom and compassion surrounding us at all times and for the various causes and conditions in our life that allow us to exist.

Sechi-ryori: Literally meaning "dishes on seasonal festive occasions" and usually referred to as *osechi-ryori*. These are the special foods eaten during the New Year. In Japan most households do not cook during the three days of the New Year celebration. Therefore, dishes are prepared beforehand to be eaten during the holidays. A formal traditional set consists of four boxes of food: the first box on top is arranged with appetizers, such as *kazunoko* (herring roe), *kuromame* (black soybeans), *tatsukuri* (small dried candied sardines), *kamaboko* (sliced fish cake), and *kinton* (smashed sweet beans of chestnuts). The second box contains broiled foods, such as *tai* (sea bream) or *ebi* (either shrimp or lobster). The third box contains *nimono* (boiled foods), such as *kobumaki* (kelp rolls) and a variety of vegetables. The fourth box contains vinegared foods, such as sushi and other delicacies.

Most of these foods symbolically represent a variety of good wishes for the New Year. For example, *kazunoko* represents prosperity for the descendants; *tatsukuri* is a homonym for cultivating the fields;

kobu rhymes with the word *yorokobu* (rejoice); and *tai* rhymes with *omede-tai* (celebration). Within most Japanese American families a combination of some or all of these foods are included with a variety of Western dishes.

Sensei: Literally meaning one who has lived before, it roughly translates as teacher. However, the title is used for doctors, teachers, priests or any respected elder.

Shochikubai: Literally means pine-bamboo-plum. This is the traditional arrangement usually placed in homes or on the altar during the New Year's holidays. Pine branches were used to represent long life, since they are evergreen. The bamboo is the symbol of endurance and resiliency since it bends but doesn't break. The plum is the first to bloom in late winter, symbolizing hardiness.

Shusho-e: This service is the first service of the year. Traditional observance of Shusho-e began in the Nara period and lasted for seven days in all the temples of Japan. These services are not a traditional part of the Jodo Shinshu tradition, since the mind of gratitude is to be expressed through the Nembutsu no matter what time of year. The New Year's Day and New Year's Eve service have become traditional parts of many Jodo Shinshu temples' observances in the United States.

Tempura: Also spelled tenpura. Japanese fritters. A batter covering a variety of foodstuffs, such as vegetables, shrimp, etc.

Toshidama: *Otoshidama* literally means "the year's gem." This is a small monetary gift given to children or young employees in small businesses on New Year's Day. Children receive it from parents or relatives when they first exchange their New Year's greetings. The custom of otoshidama developed in the late Muromachi Period where there was a custom of exchanging gifts among the nobles and samurai.

Toshikoshi Soba: Buckwheat noodles traditionally eaten on New Year's Eve. The word *soba* (buckwheat noodles) is the homophone for "close," i.e., the old year comes to a close.

Zoni: Meaning "mixed boil," also called *ozoni*. Zoni is a soup made with broth and mochi. It is a traditional soup eaten on New Year's Day morning. If the mochi stretches and sticks as you eat it, it is said to be a good omen. The ingredients vary by the area of Japan they are made in. Some areas use miso as the broth, while others will use a clear broth made from either chicken or fish. Some areas will add seafood, vegetables and other condiments.

References

Cocktails. Reverend Masao Kodani. Published by Senshin Temple Publications.

Japanese-English Dictionary of Japanese Culture. Setsuko Kojima, Gene A. Crane. Published by Heian International Inc.

Traditions of Jodoshinshu Hongwanji-ha. Reverends Masao Kodani and Russell Hamada. Published by Senshin Temple Publications.

Tikkun Olam: Repair the World

◆ ◆ ◆

Center of all centers, core of cores
almond self-enclosed and growing sweet—
all this universe, to the furthest stars
All beyond them, is your flesh, your fruit.

Now you feel how nothing clings to you;
your vast shell reaches into endless space,

and there the rich, thick fluids rise and flow.
Illuminated in our infinite peace,
a billion stars go spinning through the night,

blazing high above your head.
But in you is the presence that
will be, when all the stars are dead.

Rainer Maria Rilke, *Buddha in Glory*

Long, long ago, early in the life of the world, God formed vessels of light to hold the divine light. As he poured the divine light, the vessels shattered and these shards of light of divinity spread throughout the realm of matter. Humanity's purpose is to seek these shards of light in all things and bring them back together to "repair the world" (Tikkun Olam).

This is the time of year when most of us strive to be good little girls and good little boys—a type of self-reflection. It's a habit brought on by years and years of being bribed by Santa. Who says crime doesn't pay? As many of you know, it's one of my favorite times of the year. At the least it is a time when we can join in with others to share our mutual aspirations for Joy to the World and Peace on Earth.

I believe that we can make a difference in the world. Within the Jewish teachings this idea of repairing the world has been taught, and there are very specific teachings associated with this idea in the Lurianic Kabbalah. I like this simple idea of seeing the divine in one another as a basis for repairing or healing the world. It is what we call Buddha nature in our tradition. When we are able to recognize that you and I are the same, it helps to heal the world.

The neuroanatomist Jill Bolte Taylor has said that we human beings are over 99.9% genetically the same. I would hope that our Buddha nature, the divine light, is that 99.9%, and that it is only the one hundredth of a percent that creates the prejudice, discrimination, and bonno of the world.

There are times when I get very angry with certain situations and people at the temple. I'm sure you have each had similar experiences at your workplace. I complain to Carmela, wondering why they are so blind as to how they are hurting the Sangha with their selfishness. At the peak of this frustration, I try to remember this idea of Buddha nature within everyone. When I am confronted or usually when it slams me in the back, I have to look for that light. I may not learn to like that person, but in recognizing their 99.9% similarity to me and trying to overlook their .1% difference, I can help to repair the world.

Great change is not brought about suddenly. It is a case of gradual shifts in attitude and action. It's like your waistline, which didn't jump from 28 inches to 38 inches in a year. It took years and years of Thanksgivings, Christmases, New Years' parties and dinners. A cookie here; some nachos there. "It's Christmas. Sure, I'll have another helping." If we can each see the light in one another, we can each be a part of repairing the world, little by little.

Bodhisattvas in Our Midst

Reverently contemplating the true essence of the Pure Land way, I see that Amida's directing of virtue to sentient beings has two aspects: the aspect for our going forth to the Pure Land and the aspect for our return to this world. In the aspect for going forth, there is the true teaching, practice, shinjin, and realization.

Kyogyoshinsho, Chapter 1, *CWS*, p. 7

It was a couple of years ago that I wrote about seeing a man near Pioneer Park, dancing by himself. I believe he was probably high on drugs or alcohol. However, the feeling of exuberance and joy that I witnessed in his dancing remains with me to this day. That encounter motivated me to consider what it is that makes us happy. For us individual human beings, what constitutes our happiness? Is it money? Is it physical well being or a sense of security? What makes us happy?

In a similar manner, when I was in the Philippines, I met a small boy dressed in ragged clothes, possibly five or six years old, begging for money on the street. I didn't understand what he was saying. He spoke very quietly in Tagalog, looking up at me with sad and weary eyes. I asked my niece Christine what he was saying and she said he was asking for a few pesos. I was about to give him 100 pesos, equivalent to $2.00 in American money, and she told me that it wasn't a good idea because it only encouraged him to beg and if we gave him money, others would soon follow us around.

That encounter still plays over and over in my mind—not just about giving him the money, but the suffering of this child. I understand the logic of not encouraging his begging and how it may only add to his suffering in the long term. However, I keep thinking about how it would have probably made him extremely happy that day. I can still feel the sadness that flowed from his eyes. How much happiness has that little boy had in his life?

Both the dancing man who was possibly high on drugs and the little boy in need have enabled me to look deeper into myself. On the surface I know that they are separate from me. There is a physical distance between us. I will call them "the other." Martin Buber, the famous Jewish philosopher, describes this relationship as "I" and "it."

The man in the park and the boy on the street are merely objects perceived by me. They are not in a true relationship to me, merely objects for my own use. I evaluate these objects in relation to what benefit they have for me. In a spiritual sense the child and the man and I are the same. It is my moving beyond the perception of these two fellow beings as things or objects. This is what Buber refers to as a relationship of "I" and "thou" or "I" and "you." It is authentic and real, rather than merely an objectification of the other.

We may call this a true sense of ecology with the world around us.

In common usage, the word ecology usually refers to something environmentally friendly or merely looking at the natural environment. I believe that true ecology is when we can see the entire world in a relationship with ourselves with mutual benefit, an interdependence between you and me.

The passage I began this month's article with is from the "Chapter on Teaching" in Shinran's *Kyogyoshinsho*. I am reminded of this passage as a result of a seminar I attended at the BCA National Council Meeting. The Institute of Buddhist Studies put on this seminar. A number of speakers spoke on the topic of "Shinjin." Rev. David Matsumoto's presentation was on "the other," a short synopsis of what is also called monster theory.

After his talk I was asking him how he came across this monster theory, or other theory. He said it was from a discussion with a Ryukoku University professor who referred to his son David, who has Down syndrome, as a Bodhisattva having returned from the Pure Land (*genso bosatsu*). The idea of returning from the Pure Land, also called *genso eko* is from this passage written by Shinran. Those who return from the Pure Land are the Bodhisattvas playing in the ocean of birth and death.

We all have a tendency to view people, places and things around us as objects that are to be used for our personal needs. This is the relationship of "I" and "it." In many ways it is a necessary aspect for survival. It is easier for me to live with perceiving a wild man on the street or a ragged homeless boy as something far removed from my own existence. They are the monsters in the closet. In a similar manner, our relationship with the environment is as though it were merely for our personal comfort. We switch on the air conditioning or heater because it's too hot or too cold, regardless of the effect to the present or future world. In either case, this sense of entitlement is a result of our bonno.

It is my hope that through our continued hearing of the Dharma, we may move beyond our "I" and "it" relationships with the world around us and into an "I" and "thou" relationship. Whether it concerns personal or societal relationships or the environment or ecology, it is how we perceive and act in this dance of life. When I am allowed to look through the cracks of my own bonno and see the monsters in the closet, I can begin to see that I am surrounded by the music of the Pure Land and am in the midst of Bodhisattvas.

Life Swiftly Passes

◆ ◆ ◆

"Kalamas, when you yourselves know: 'These things are good; these things are not blamable; these things are praised by the wise; undertaken and observed, these things lead to benefit and happiness,' enter on and abide in them."

Kalama Sutra

A couple of weeks ago, I was driving with my daughter Taylor, and she asked me, "Dad, have you ever wanted to go back in time?"

I thought about it for a moment and told her, "Not really. If I went back in time, I would have to go back to things I may not want to go through again. I'd rather just be grateful for the things I have now and keep on going. Why, Tay? Do you want to go back in time?"

"Yeah, I would. Just to see what it is that I've been doing."

"What do you mean?" I asked.

"You know…it seems that I'm so busy every day just living my life that I don't have time to really see what I'm doing. Two years just fly by without me getting to really understand what is going on around or in myself. I'd like to understand my life and what I'm doing a little better. So I'd like to go back in time to at least see where I've been, to know what to do now." I felt like putting my hands in gassho and bowing to her, but I was driving.

It's taken me fifty years to come to some sense of the swift passage of time, and Taylor is eight years old. I read about it in every book on Buddhism. Life is impermanent and forever changing. Rennyo Shonin has written in his letter "On White Ashes" which I read at each funeral, "When we contemplate the transient nature of human life, we conclude that this fleeting life of ours from beginning to end is like an illusion." One of the facts of this life is that one day each of us will die. Yet we live as though we will be the exception. I am no exception to this!

There is a quote I like from Taisen Deshimaru, a famous Soto Zen Roshi, "Time is not a line, but a series of now points." He also said, "To receive everything, one must open one's hands and give." But that's another Dharma talk. The first quote reminds us how he believes we should look at life, not as a continuous line or one line of drudgery, but as a series of now moments. To do this allows us to examine life, or rather to fully live. Most of us live as Taylor said, quickly moving forward without taking the time to observe what we are doing. If we can learn to appreciate this moment and savor it with our entire being, we will know the infinite past and what and where we are going in the future.

The other day during our Sunday study class, the question was brought up about why we meditate at a Jodo Shinshu temple. Traditionally, Jodo Shinshu temples do not have meditation. I believe that one reason is that our teaching emphasizes the efficacy of Amida Buddha's Primal Vow and that the Great Practice is that which has been completed by Amida Buddha, rather than our depending upon our own weak forms of practice based upon ego.

However, the practical reason for not having meditation is that the original Jodo Shinshu Buddhists were the peasants of Japan. These were the workers who got up early in the morning and got home late at night, barely able to do anything other than try to scrape a living for their family. As Taylor said, "I'm so busy everyday living my life, that I don't have time to really see what I'm doing." Meditation was a luxury that few could afford. Jodo Shinshu's teaching expressed and taught them that they were okay just as they were, and to express appreciation was all that was needed.

I believe that in some ways we are like those peasants in our spiritual abilities. However, the majority of us at the Salt Lake Buddhist Temple do have some free time to figure out what we are doing with our lives. I believe that a short period of meditation helps to clear away a bit of the illusions and delusions of this life. It is good to bring a bit of clarity into our otherwise busy and chaotic lives. I hope you will join us for one or all of our services.

I began this article with a quote from the Kalama Sutra where Shakyamuni Buddha explained to the Kalama clan how to determine if a teaching was right for them. I would like to recommend that you also follow how to determine if something is not right or proper for you:

> It is proper for you, Kalamas, to doubt, to be uncertain; uncertainty has arisen in you about what is doubtful. Come, Kalamas. Do not go upon what has been acquired by repeated hearing; nor upon tradition; nor upon rumor; nor upon what is in a scripture; nor upon surmise; nor upon an axiom; nor upon specious reasoning; nor upon a bias towards a notion that has been pondered over; nor upon another's seeming ability; nor upon the consideration, "The monk is our teacher." Kalamas, when you yourselves know: "These things are bad; these things are blamable; these things are censured by the wise; undertaken and observed, these things lead to harm and ill," abandon them.

Trick or Treat and Namo Amida Butsu

◆ ◆ ◆

I will have no regrets even though I should have been deceived by Honen Shonin and thus by uttering the Nembutsu, I should fall into hell. The reason is that, if I could become Buddha by performing some other practice and fell into hell uttering the Nenbutsu, then, I might feel regret at having been deceived. But since I am incapable of any practice whatsoever, hell would definitely be my dwelling anyway.

Tannisho, Chapter 2

It was cold enough so that before I left the house, Mom called out, "You'd better wear your jacket and be careful."

I thought to myself, "Yeah right, on Halloween? Forget the jacket." I called back to her, "Thanks, Mom. Don't worry, I'll see you later. Bye." Richard and Brian were already waiting for me at the corner. We had perfected our trick-or-treating skills over the years, to the point that we could cover almost two miles in about three hours.

We had been working the neighborhood for about half an hour. I looked deep into my white pillowcase. Over the years I had started using a pillowcase rather than those little orange plastic pumpkins or colorful shopping bags with the Halloween faces painted on them. Pillowcases held at least three times as much as the pumpkins and didn't tear like the shopping bags. I easily spotted my latest acquisition at the top of the pile and pulled out the Tootsie Pop. Richard and Brian came up and asked in unison, "Hey, Jerry, what'd you get?" This was a part of the ritual. After every house we would compare notes on what we had received, assuming that one of us might get something better than the others.

"A Tootsie Pop," I announced, pulling off the wrapper and popping it into my mouth.

"Yeah? Same here," sighed Richard.

"Well, I guess that's better than the last house," chirped in Brian.

"You mean where that old lady was giving out one Hershey kiss,"

I responded.

"Yeah," said Brian. "And on top of that she wanted us to sing a song. Jeez. What's she think this is? Eugene Jelesnick's Talent Show?"

Richard and I nodded in agreement. "I know what ya mean. I really hate those houses with the women that kinda screech, 'Ohh…how cute! Honey, come out and see these kids and bring the camera.' Then they take your picture and give you a handful of that old candy corn," I said, shaking my head in disgust.

It was still early. The three of us had only covered about half a mile. At the next house, we each received a sloppy looking popcorn ball and it wasn't even wrapped—a definite candidate for the garbage can. "Man, at least they could have wrapped it," I said. "Don't they know our moms won't let us eat that kind of stuff?" The three of us, somewhat disappointed, started out for the next house. "Well, I guess this is as good a time as any," I mysteriously sighed.

"What you talkin' about, Jerry?" asked Richard.

"Well, I heard that on Wilson Avenue there's a guy giving out candy apples. Not those cheap jobbies that those people make with a Popsicle stick—an old apple and some melted caramel—but the real ones. You know, the red candy ones, in a plastic container with the nuts on it."

"WOW!" said Brian and Richard. "Let's go!" We received two candy apples each. The houses with the really good stuff deserved two visitations. We'd naturally wait a while before returning. I always felt a little guilty about going back to the same house. A couple of times I'd back out. But I hated being called "CHICKEN." So, I would usually follow what my friends did, even if I knew deep down that it wasn't right.

A few months later on the day after Christmas, Brian and Richard came over to my house. "What'd you get, Jerry?" asked Richard.

"Well, boys, Santa was really good to me. I guess it was because I'm so kind and gentle to every living thing," I said in a gloating manner.

"What are you talking about?" asked Brian.

"I got a Johnny Seven multi-purpose action gun and an army uniform with real patches!"

"WOW!" they both yelled. "I guess Joni didn't tell your mom or dad about your little soda shampoo for her Barbie doll," said Brian.

"Shhh…my mom and dad are in the other room," I cautioned.

"I'll be quiet if you let me shoot your Johnny Seven," said Brian.

"All right, but you'd better not lose any of the missiles."

"I know, I know," said Brian. "I'll be careful." Then they would tell me what they had received from Santa. This went on year after year, until we slowly drifted apart.

These little incidents happened over forty years ago. It was a time when my friends and I would compare our latest possessions. "What'd you get?" was a question we'd ask after Halloween, birthdays, Christmases and various other occasions. Looking back to this time in my life, I realize that the candy apples and Johnny Sevens of my youth were wonderful treasures. However, they were very temporary treasures. The candy apples would be eaten before Halloween night was over. My Johnny Seven would eventually lose all its red missiles and the secret handgun to boot. These seeming treasures are now only fond memories. Even my friendships with Brian and Richard had faded over the years.

However, the little lessons that I learned in Dharma school, such as "I will try to be kind and gentle to every living thing" or the conscience that made me feel guilty for taking two candy apples continue to be important treasures in my life and remain with me to this day. It is something that I now have the opportunity to pass on to my own daughter, even though I realize Kacie probably wouldn't even like my Johnny Seven gun or grocery-store-bought candy apple.

The friendships that I had during my youth, those from the old neighborhood, are only fond memories, like Halloween candy and wonderful Christmas presents of years gone by. It's funny, the one thing I was often a little hesitant about comparing with my friends is something that I have found to be among my most treasured possessions. That was and is my religious beliefs. My friends would talk about Sunday school. I would often shy away from the subject, fearing ridicule for being different. I wish Richard or Brian could now ask me, "What'd you get, Jerry?"

Children often compare their own standing in the world with what their friends have in comparison to themselves. As adults, we do the same thing. We compare jobs, salaries, positions, houses, etc. Living in Utah, we are often asked, "Oh, you're Buddhist? What do you do as a Buddhist?" It's a similar question to "What'd you get?" If my old friends were to ask me about what I had received, I could now proudly answer, "I have received a teaching that allows me to truly be myself. It allows me to exist with all other beings, in harmony with all things. I have learned about gratitude for Amida Buddha's wondrous compassion that extends to all of us. This is a treasure that I can share with you. Would you like to try it?"

If you were asked, "What'd you get?" how would you respond? This is a question that each of us could reflect upon. Namo Amida Butsu.

Gratitude and Impermanence

You are fooled by your mind into believing there is tomorrow, so you may waste today.

Ishin Yoshimoto, founder of Naikan

Our family had just returned from our yearly vacation. As we drove up the driveway, I was amazed at the number of leaves that had fallen while we were gone. The leaves were an inch thick over much of the front yard. The leaves had filled our pond in the rear of the house, stopping the flow of water. Although I know that with the autumn season come cooler temperatures and the falling leaves, it was still somewhat of a shock.

We had just returned from Florida where the temperatures were in the mid to upper eighties and the humidity quite high. Suddenly, Carmela and I were in the backyard of our home with the temperature in the forties, on our hands and knees, scooping out leaves from the pond and the filter system and trying to bring back the flow of water to the pond and our lives.

As the flow to the pond and our lives returned to a somewhat orderly manner and we had settled back into the house, I had the opportunity to reflect on the various changes that had occurred over the past week. Our trip was extremely busy and at times stressful. I don't know about other families, but when our entire family travels together, there are always stressful situations and arguments of one sort or the other. This trip was no exception. Along with Carmela, Taylor and me (Kacie could not make the trip because of her dance practices), Katie, Carmela's 19-year-old daughter; her sister and brother-in-law from the Philippines, Ada and Roy; and my cousin Mike with his wife Connie and their son Garrett had lived together for one week at Disney World.

Now that I was home and the cold water from the pond had shocked my brain, I was able to reflect on the various interactions between Carmela and myself and how they had changed and even broken down at times. From my ego-centered perspective, I had to adjust to all of the new roles we were thrust into. During the trip, Carmela was no longer just my wife and partner, but Katie's mother, Taylor's stepmother, Roy and Ada's little sister, and Mike, Connie and Garrett's in-law. Although I know that in theory she wears many hats, there is a very self-centered part of me that just wants her to center her life as my wife and partner. When things change, it is very difficult for my ego to adjust, and as a result, everyone suffers. We do not exist in a vacuum; when we are selfish, all others around us suffer the consequences of those self-centered actions.

As a human being, one of the things that we each long for is unconditional love. When we are babies, it is our parents that usually supply this embrace. To paraphrase one of Shinran Shonin's poems: "If we see the Buddha as we see our mothers, we will meet the Buddha in the present life or our near future." I believe that in this poem Shinran is addressing our search for unconditional love.

In this world, I do not believe we will find unconditional love with another human being. The relationship between husbands and wives and relatives and friends will change. To retain our sense of love within each of these relationships, there are conditions that must be met. Even the relationship between parent and child can be tested and strained if the right conditions are not met. The only unconditional love that I believe is available to each of us is that love with Amida Buddha. Without a sense of self-reflection, even this may be a one-sided relationship—Amida Buddha to us.

So what is the condition that can maintain the love in the relationships with others in our lives? I feel that we may find and nurture this love if we understand gratitude and develop a true sense of it in our lives. The passage I began this article with is by Ishin Yoshimoto, the founder of Naikan. Naikan is a Japanese word that means "looking inside." Greg Krech, an authority on Naikan, has called it, "seeing oneself with the mind's eye."

Yoshimoto was a devout Jodo Shinshu Buddhist, whose deep religious spirit led him to practice *mishirabe* (self examination), a very arduous and difficult method of meditation and self-reflection. Realizing that most people could not follow this form, he developed Naikan so that it could be more widely practiced. Our ego puts our view of life into a zoom lens. I have a tendency to focus on my needs and how they are being met. I am the center of the world and others are there to meet my needs. Naikan allows me to switch to a wide-angle lens. My perspective is still a part of the view, but I am enabled to witness the amazing world of compassion that is surrounding me.

Naikan is very simple in method. It focuses on three questions: What have I received from _____? What have I given to _____? What troubles and difficulties have I caused _____? During a Naikan seminar, you are asked to meditate on these three questions, focusing on an individual or even the world around you and to list the answers you find. For example, What have I received from Carmela?

What have I given to Carmela? What troubles and difficulties have I caused Carmela?

Yoshimoto was a businessman who realized that just as he sent out statements to his customers and received similar statements from his suppliers, he could conduct an audit of his life, seeing the debts he had accrued against those that were owed to him. He realized that he was in the red concerning that which he owed the world.

I believe that instead of living as though the world owes us, most of us will find that we, too, are in debt for what we have received. With this type of self-reflection we can instill within ourselves a realistic sense of gratitude and humility. Our lives continue to flow. Our relationships change within this river of time. We can never step into the same place again. At least we can be grateful for the embracing lives and causes and conditions that allow us to step into the stream. Namo Amida Butsu.

Kosher Teriyaki?

◆◆◆

First [realizing] the settled mind in our tradition does not mean that we put a stop to our mind's evil or to the rising of delusions and attachments. Simply carry on your trade or position of service, hunt, and fish. For when we realize deeply that Amida Tathagata's Primal Vow promises to save such worthless beings as ourselves, confused morning and evening by evil karma when we single-heartedly rely on the compassionate Vow of the one Buddha Amida, and when sincere faith is awakened in us with the realization that Amida saves us then without fail we partake of the Tathagata's saving work.

Beyond this, when there is a question as to with what understanding we should say the Nembutsu, [the answer is that] we are to say the Nembutsu as long as we live, realizing that it is in gratitude, in return for the gracious benevolence that saves us by giving us the power of entrusting, through which our birth is assured. [Those who do] this are to be called practicers of faith, in whom the settled mind of our tradition is established.

Letters of Rennyo: 1-3, "On Hunting and Fishing"

Every fall, my parents would take my sister and me to the fair. It was something I looked forward to with great anticipation. My sister will often say that much of the time my family spent at the fair was looking for me after I had wandered off and gotten lost in the crowd. My response is that the active mind of an intellectually searching, inquisitive child will naturally find the fair fascinating. The smells of the popcorn, cotton candy, corn dogs and candy apples, accompanied by the bright lights and music swirling about the midway, along with the beckoning call of the multitude of vendors hawking their wares, was as great a lure as the Sirens' call to Ulysses' sailors. In other words, I just couldn't help myself. That is why I never let Kacie out of my sight when we go to the fair.

The midway and souvenir stands were the high point of my visits to the fair. Next on my list would be the artwork, food displays, produce and handicrafts. However, the livestock exhibits were definitely at the bottom of my list of must-see fair attractions. Being from the city, the smells of slowly decaying hay, feed, manure, and the animals themselves often resulted in my gasping for air by the end of the exhibition hall. Even the exhibitors themselves seemed a little suspicious to me. How could anyone set up a bed among the hay and take a nap amid that smell? Most of the men and women were also extremely big and muscular. As a child looking at these imposing figures, dressed in their tight jeans, pointy boots, large hats and funny colored shirts, I could imagine them easily hog-tying me and cooking me at their leisure. Give me the midway and the colorful lifestyle of the carnies any day. There were times when I even fantasized about leading the life of a carnie, traveling around the country, running the games or maybe one of the large midway rides, and eating corn dogs and candy apples whenever I wanted. What a life.

My children's mother, Cheryl, was not raised in the city. She had been a member of the 4-H Club while in school. Seeing the huge assortment of farm animals is for her a trip down memory lane. As a result, she makes it a point that we take Kacie to all the livestock exhibits. I manage to somehow make it through the cows, bunnies, chickens, sheep and smaller livestock. However, I usually have to pass on the pigs.

Cheryl, Kacie and our niece Shelby happily went into the pig exhibit. I sat and waited a slight distance away. When they re-emerged, Kacie came running up to me, excitedly explaining her new discovery of seeing a mother pig sleeping with her piglets. Cheryl somewhat self-satisfactorily said, "See how educational these exhibits are? Look what you missed out on." I explained, "That's why we collect beanie babies. Kacie gets to see all kinds of animals and we don't have to go to the barn to see them." Cheryl just looked at me and shook her head.

As we walked to the midway and food booths, Shelby asked, "Uncle Jerry, what do we get from the animals?" I explained that we get milk and beef from the cows, wool from the sheep, poultry and eggs from the chickens, and bacon and hot dogs from the pigs. Once again, Cheryl enthusiastically told the girls how educational the livestock exhibits were and how coming to the fair wasn't just riding rides, playing games and eating corn dogs and cotton candy. I tried to think of a clever retort but realized she was right.

Later in the afternoon, as I was biting into Kacie's leftover corn dog, I realized how all those things that had been somewhat abhorrent to my citified senses were in reality things that sustained my life. Those scary ranchers and farmers making their living amid that smell I could barely breathe in were supporting my life. If they didn't do what they did, I would not have my beloved cheeseburgers, fries, pizzas or any other food and drink. Even much of the clothing I wore was a result of their hard and honest labor. How many other things do I take for granted and even stay away from that in reality allow me to live my chosen lifestyle?

The passage I began this essay with is from Rennyo Shonin's *Gobunsho*. In many sects of Buddhism, harming or the taking of life is considered a grave karmic condition with various negative results. There are many rules of conduct that forbid or suggest not eating meat if at all possible. As a result, those who hunted or fished or whose livelihood depended upon such things were often looked down upon as lower class people. In this letter, I interpret Rennyo to be saying that each of us—no matter what type of lifestyle we live—takes part in these karmic evils. It is only through Amida Buddha's compassion that we are released from the karmic consequences.

However, this does not release us from the fact that we do cause suffering to other sentient beings. Our lives are a compromise with our knowing that we are causing this suffering, yet enjoying the fruits of the lives and labor of others. Within the Jewish religious tradition, they have the laws of kosher. Within this tradition eating meat is a moral compromise.

There is great misunderstanding about the Jewish laws that consider certain foods to be kosher. Some have said that these laws are a result of health concerns—that not eating pork is a result of concern about trichinosis or contamination. This is the same for certain shellfish. Rabbi Harold Kushner, in his book *To Life!*, denies these assertions. He suggests that the laws of kosher have everything to do with taking the process of eating, which we share with all other animals, and making it a uniquely human activity by investing it with considerations of permitted and forbidden. He says there is a difference between eating a bowl of cereal and eating a hamburger. In eating a hamburger, the cow had to die. I would have to agree.

In Jodo Shinshu, we do not have kosher laws for the things we eat. As a result, we eat whatever we want. However, we do encourage everyone to say "Namo Amida Butsu, *Itadakimasu*" and "Namo Amida Butsu, *Gochisosama.*" These short but simple phrases are for us to understand the sacrifices that were given so that we can enjoy the foods we are about to eat.

Itadakimasu, literally means to place something on the top of one's head. This is an expression of gratitude and humility for the food that we are about to partake of. In the word, Gochisosama, "*Go*" is an honorific, "*chi*" is the character for "rushing on horseback," and "*so*" is the character for "running on foot." This symbolizes our gratitude for all those who rushed around so that we could have the food we eat.

Although they may be short and very simple things, saying "Namo Amida Butsu, Itadakimasu" and "Namo Amida Butsu, Gochisosama" provides us with a huge difference in understanding the interdependence of all living things. As Rabbi Kushner says, "Should we ever become so casual about the eating of meat that we lose sight of that distinction, a part of our humanity will have shriveled and died." To understand our humanity is a large part of understanding Jodo Shinshu.

I feel that these ideas of kosher are wonderful in making one aware of the gratitude we should feel for the foods that sustain us. At the bazaars of all the temples within the BCA, how many types of food are served? It is my hope that all the bazaars that we undertake are successful. However, even more important, I hope that all of us that partake of the benefits of the wonderful food realize the sacrifice of so much time, effort, and things—both animate and inanimate—which allow us to live. Although we do not have laws for keeping our foods kosher, let us try to be aware of what we are doing when eating—a sort of kosher teriyaki chicken.

Rain of Compassion

◆ ◆ ◆

I am the Thus Come One, most honored of two-legged beings. I appear in the world like a great cloud that showers moisture upon all the dry and withered living beings, so that all are able to escape suffering, gain the joy of peace and security, the joys of this world, and the joy of nirvana. All you heavenly and human beings of this assembly, listen carefully and with one mind!

Lotus Sutra, Chapter 5

Now that spring has arrived, my allergies are in full bloom. As I look at the beautiful blossoms in the trees surrounding my home or the various flowers that are beginning to show themselves in the flower beds, I enjoy them for only a split second before I have to rub the junk out of my eyes or blow my dripping nose. As I step outside and smell the blossoming landscape, I feel the chafe around my nostrils. There is a part of me that enjoys the spring and another part that curses the same things that give me enjoyment in the spring. It is a world of contradiction. I need the Dharma Rain to water the seeds of goodness within me rather than allow myself to water the seeds of evil, which seem to come so naturally to me.

I have never been a person who is naturally good. When I look back at my life, I find that the so-called "dark side" has fascinated me more than the "force side," which I express in the vernacular of *Star Wars*. It sounds surprising that someone who has chosen my particular profession as a Buddhist priest would be fascinated by evil rather than good. Actually, someone who is naturally evil, like me, can probably appreciate how strong compassion can be in our life, since I see it on a daily basis. My natural intentions of moving towards the "dark side" are rewarded with good. It is only as a result of the good around me that I have been allowed to become a Buddhist priest. There are people I have met who are naturally good and cheerful. My wife Carmela is someone that I have found to be naturally good. My friend

80

Rev. Marvin Harada is a person I know to be a naturally good person.

Both of them look towards goodness in people. They believe that people have good intentions. They both rarely complain about what others have done to them. When they become upset, I know that they first look at what they could have done to bring about those feelings of animosity. These negative feelings are a result of something they did to someone else rather than something that someone else has done to them. Unlike them, I would first blame the other person. When I feel bad, I look to see who is disturbing my tranquility with his or her ego. It is in my nature to complain or become upset by others and not look to my own ego first. My life has been blessed with having people such as Carmela and Rev. Harada surrounding me, reminding me about the goodness in this world. It is as a result of these types of individuals that I have become a priest; it is as a result of these people that I live.

When I was in high school and at the University of Utah, the movies *Godfather I, II* and *III* came out. I thought that I would love to be a *consigliere* for the Mafia. Tom Hagen, played by Robert Duvall, was the consigliere for Don Corleone. I imagined how fun it would be to be an outlaw, playing the legal system for the benefit of my "family." Tom Hagen wasn't evil enough; I identified more with Sonny Corleone, who became the wartime consigliere for the Corleone family. I felt more in common with Sonny than his pacifist brother Michael. It thrilled me when Michael finally realized his destiny to become the Godfather as he allowed his evil side to fully blossom. In some ways, he was my ideal.

The older I have gotten, the more I see how my ego, my bonno, has created suffering in my life and in the lives of those around me. There are things that have happened in my life that I would never want to live through again. However, it is these dark times that have taught me how lucky I am with the majority of my life. These dark places have taught me to enjoy what I have. The evil I know that is a part of who I am has not been allowed to bloom. Various bodhisattvas in my life have watered the true Buddha nature within me.

The other day, Taylor asked me what makes me sad. I couldn't think of anything in particular and I asked her what made her sad. She told me the saddest part of her life was Mondays and Wednesdays when I took her home to her mom's house and Tuesdays and Thursdays when she didn't get to see me. It had nothing to do with her mom, for I know how much Taylor loves her. It was just the separation and saying goodbye and not seeing each other in the morning that hurt. She felt the same way when she was with me and missed her mom. After I kissed Taylor goodbye and good night, she went into her mom's house. As I drove out of the driveway and started home, I saw her open the balcony door. I stopped in the road and opened the window of my car. She shouted, "I love you, Dad! Thanks! Good night."

When I pulled up into the driveway of my house, I felt a peace come over me. It was strange because I was feeling sad about Taylor's predicament. Yet, seeing the lights in my home, I realized how really content I was with my life. I was at a place in my life that I never would have imagined I would be because of the fact that I was returning to a home that belonged to Carmela and me. Although Taylor's sadness bothered me, I knew I could discuss those feelings of dismay with Carmela. My divorce from Taylor's mom had brought about Taylor's sadness. However, without having gone through that divorce, I would never have met Carmela. Without having been married to Taylor's mom, I would never have had Taylor or Kacie. I also knew that Taylor and Kacie have parents who love them very much.

I realize that these contradictory feelings—happiness and sadness, and good and evil—are a part of life. It made me see that an evil person like me can still be surrounded with compassion. Each of us has the possibility of good and evil. They are both aspects of who we are. I believe there are some who are more susceptible toward evil than good. The amazing aspect in life is that compassion surrounds both. Just as the spring rain waters the flowers in the garden, it also waters the weeds. The sun shines on both, as does Amida Buddha's compassion that rains upon us all. Namo Amida Butsu.

A Sufi Jewish Buddhist Tale

◆ ◆ ◆

The Nasrudin stories are known throughout the Middle East and have touched cultures around the world. Superficially, most of the Nasrudin stories may be told as jokes or humorous anecdotes. They are told and retold endlessly in the teahouses and caravanserais of Asia and can be heard in homes and on the radio. But it is inherent in a Nasrudin story that it may be understood at many levels. There is the joke, followed by a moral — and usually the little extra, which brings the consciousness of the potential mystic a little further on the way to realization.

The Sufis Idries Shah (from Wikipedia)

I would like to begin this article with a Sufi story I heard from Mark Epstein. He is a Jewish man who writes about and practices Buddhist psychiatry. He has studied a great deal about Buddhism and regards Jack Kornfield, Joseph Goldstein, Stephen Batchelor and many other Buddhist teachers and scholars as his teachers. From what I have read, he does not identify his Buddhism with any particular sect. This story I want to tell you is written in a couple of his books, but I can't remember if I first heard it at a talk of his that I attended or if I read it in one of his books. To my memory it is probably a little of both.

This is a story about a man named Nasrudin. As the short quote I began with explains, Nasrudin (sometimes spelled Nasruddin) stories are told throughout the Middle East. They were originally about a real man born in the Middle East in the 13th century. Within the Sufi tradition, he is usually a combination of wise man and fool. In Jodo Shinshu we often have similar stories about people we call *Myokonin*. Over the centuries there came to be many various stories about Nasrudin and I believe Nasrudin could represent any of us human beings.

In this story we find Nasrudin on his hands and knees in the village square. He seems to be searching for something, crawling around under a street light. Some villagers see Nasrudin and ask him, "Nasrudin, what are you doing? Did you lose something?" He answers, "Yes, I lost my key and I can't seem to find it anywhere." One of the villagers asks him, "Did you lose your key here in the square?" Nasrudin answers, "No, I lost it at home." The villager questions him, "Then why are you looking here when you lost your key at home?" Nasrudin pauses and answers incredulously, "Because this area has the best light."

Mark Epstein talks about how he first heard this story from his teacher Joseph Goldstein, who used the story as an example of how people search for happiness in inherently fleeting, and therefore unsatisfactory, pleasant feelings. He himself had a number of interpretations to this story. He then talks about reading this same story in another book called *Ambivalent Zen* by Lawrence Shainberg. In this book the author talks about liking this story and asking his Japanese Zen teacher about it. I will quote from Mark Epstein's book *Going on Being*:

"You know the story about Nasruddin and the keys?" Shainberg asked his master.

"Nasruddin?" the Roshi replied. "Who is Nasruddin?"

After Shainberg described the story to him, his master appeared to give it no thought, but sometime later the Roshi brought it up again.

"So, Larry-san, what's Nasruddin saying?" the Zen master questioned his disciple.

"I asked you, Roshi."

"Easy," he said. "Looking *is* the key."

When I read this explanation, I understood the depth of Nasrudin. It wasn't in the details of how or where you got there; it was the search—the looking—that was important.

Buddhism has many different forms, and in the West many of the teachings that we hear are an amalgam of Japanese, Indian, Thai and Tibetan forms. Our temple is a Jodo Shinshu temple, which is Japanese. Jodo Shinshu has been in America for over one hundred years and there are many things that have changed to fit our American environment. At the moment there are many things that are still changing (how ridiculous to think they won't change!). As Shakyamuni Buddha advised, "Do not wish for the changing to be unchanging." I hope that our Sangha will never forget where we came from, or as the Buddha said, "How will we know where we are going?" However, even above being Japanese or Jodo Shinshu, I hope our temple will remain open-minded and learn from all traditions.

With all this in mind I would like to mention one more book that I recently read: *Outliers: The Story of Success,* written by Malcolm Gladwell. The definition for outlier is as follows:

> Outliers, noun, 1: something that is situated away from or classed differently from a main or related body; 2: a statistical observation that is markedly different in value from the others of the sample.

I first heard about this book in the discussion session of our recent Mountain States District Conference, which was so skillfully and successfully chaired by Reiko Mitsunaga. In the beginning of the book the author writes about a small Pennsylvanian town named Roseto. He writes how scientists first began studying this small town because of a chance encounter with one physician, who said that it seemed as though the residents of Roseto didn't suffer from heart disease. They did a study of the town and found that this was true.

Scientists then began to try to find out why the Rosetans differed from their neighbors. Was it the food? The air? The water? What was it that made life less stressful for the Rosetans?

In their studies they found that it was none of these outside factors. For the Rosetans, it wasn't the diet, the physical environment, the exercise or genes that made the difference in their lives. The difference was in the community they had created for themselves. It was their sharing of life with one another during happy and sad times. The feeling of being embraced by their community was what made the difference. I would like to believe that our small Jodo Shinshu temple at the base of the Wasatch Mountains can become an outlier from other Sanghas within the BCA and America in general; a place that creates a powerful, protective social structure capable of insulating us from the pressures of the modern world. It would be a place that supports and encourages us, not flaunting our successes and not pointing at our failures.

If you have been wondering what these two stories have to do with each other, I would like to offer you my wish for our Sangha and explain why it is so important. The story of Nasrudin reminded me of another story of Shakyamuni Buddha. A disciple once asked the Buddha about the status of the Sangha in his teachings. In other words, how important was the Sangha in understanding the teaching? The Buddha replied, "It is *everything*."

Nasrudin's searching for his keys was not so much about the keys, but the search itself was the key. I believe in a similar manner that there are many who believe that the Sangha must remain solely defined by the type of teaching or sect of Buddhism taught there and that the goal is to remain solely within the confines of that sect or Sangha. There may have been a time when I agreed. However, I have definitely strayed from this path. In terms of universal truth, these are much too confining parameters.

Buddhism is about learning universal truth, not just what a particular sect or religion teaches. With such a narrow-minded interpretation many are misunderstanding the Sangha and misconstruing its true nature. Truth cannot be defined in simple Jodo Shinshu, Tibetan, Zen, Buddhist, Jewish or Sufi terms. As in the Nasrudin story with the Zen master, Sangha may be the key, but Buddhism is life itself.

Sickness

When I was younger, I thought the worst type of sickness was that of the body. Over the past few years, I have had cancer, shoulder and knee surgeries and even died in a hospital in Reno, Nevada from internal bleeding. Physical illnesses can teach you, but I have found the worst type of sickness is that of the mind: bigotry, discrimination, greed, anger and ignorance, what Buddhists call Klesha *or* Bonno.

Rodney's Heart

◆ ◆ ◆

Living the truth in your heart without compromise brings kindness into the world. Attempts at kindness that compromise your heart cause only sadness.

Anonymous

One very cold and snowy morning, as I rang the daikin to begin the morning service, I heard a slight rattling in front of the door that leads into the hondo. I began chanting and heard the front door of the temple open and someone walk in. As I chanted, I watched the entrance to the hondo to see who might have come in. Slowly, a man bundled in layers of coats and clothes, with an old knit cap over his long hair and carrying a large duffel bag, looked into the hondo. It was hard to see his face, for he had a long tangled beard.

As I continued chanting, I watched him shed gloves, cap, bag and topcoat. He kind of shook himself off and walked into the hondo and towards the altar. He bowed to me and then quietly sat in the front pew. While I chanted, I occasionally glanced at this stranger. The snow dripped from his beard and boots, making a small dirty puddle of water at his feet. As I wondered what this rather bedraggled man was doing in the hondo, I heard a thumping sound. I looked up and he was hitting the side of his head with an open hand. Water scattered from his head with each strike. It was as if he was trying to clear his head of some unknown pain. I ended the service and I walked from the naijin and introduced myself, "My name is Jerry Hirano. Is there something I can do for you?" He stood up, bowed and said, "I heard the bell and thought I should come in for *sesshin*." *Sesshin* literally means "collecting the heart-mind." It is a time for especially intensive and strict practice

89

of collected meditation and discussion carried out in Zen monasteries at regular intervals.

I walked towards him and put out my hand saying, "This is a Jodo Shinshu temple and we don't follow Zen practice, but you're welcome to the services we do have. Have you been studying Zen very long?" As he took my hand, he said, "My name's Rodney. That's okay. I haven't formally studied Buddhism." I was surprised by how his hand felt as I shook it. From the way he was dressed in his raggedy clothes, I expected a cold, calloused hand. However, although dirty, his hand was very warm and soft. He continued talking, "I travel around a lot and thought I should come in to talk with and join you, when I heard the bell."

"Well, Rodney, that's basically all I do in the morning," I told him. He looked cold and as though he had not eaten for a while, so I offered him some tea. "I don't have any coffee or anything to eat. But would you like to join me for some tea? We can talk in the kitchen while the water is boiling." He paused for a moment, stood there looking at the ground, and said, "Sure. I'd like that."

As I walked back to the naijin to put out the candles and lights, I saw him look into the *osaisen* bowl that we have near the incense burners. I thought he might take the few dollars that were there. I knew there were only a couple dollars in there, so I thought, "If he takes the couple dollars, I won't say anything. He probably needs it more than this temple does." Instead of taking the money, he fumbled through the layers of clothes he was wearing and pulled out a beat-up wallet and pulled out a crumpled dollar bill. It looked as though it was his only dollar. He then bowed and gently placed it in the bowl.

I turned out the lights in the naijin and we walked to the kitchen. I put water in the kettle and looked through the cabinets for some tea. Out of the corner of my eyes, I saw Rodney moving around, as though he were practicing some kung fu moves he must have seen in a movie or television show. As he looked upwards, he kind of froze and stood there posed, staring up into space. I broke the silence by saying, "Well, Rodney, where are you from? Do you live around here?"

I think I startled him out of his thoughts, for he jerked back into standing there with his arms hanging at his sides. He thought for a minute and said, "Well, I live all over the place. I like to move 'round."

"Where were you born?"

"I was born in Los Angeleez and been moving 'round for 'bout seven years." As he spoke, I looked closely at his face. Beneath the beard and the grime, I could tell that he must be younger than I was. If he had been moving around for at least seven years, he must have left home as a teenager or in his early twenties.

"I've lived all over, Florida, Looziana, Texas.... Let's see, Wyoming, Arizona and I've been in Denver for the past six months."

"Isn't it cold here in Utah?"

"I don't mind. I like to travel around."

"Where did you hear about sesshin, if you haven't studied Zen?"

"I don't have any religion. When I travel 'round, I stop here and there and listen. Heard folks talkin' 'bout Zen and say sesshin. I try to go to the Christian churches, too." He looked at me as if to apologize.

"It's all right. We all have to find our own paths. Whether you're Buddhist or Christian doesn't matter to me. All of us have to find out what it means to be human."

"I agree. I'm still looking for my path."

"Me too," I said to him.

He kind of smiled at me and said, "The last church I was in was a Catholic Church in Denver. It was nice there, but I like to move 'round." He seemed to be remembering some happy moments in his past as he said this. I then offered him some tea, which he accepted and drank. He then asked me, "What do you think it means to be human?" I began to explain to him the ideas of bonno and how we are all filled with these passions, characterized by greed, anger and ignorance. Rodney attentively listened to what I was saying and looked at my *onenju*. I explained why I have an onenju. He said, "That's kinda like a rosary, isn't it?"

"That's right." I responded.

He then said he had something he felt that he could now show me and he pulled out a little pouch from his pocket. In the pouch were three dirty crystals. I asked him, "Did you find those in your travels?"

"No, I bought them in Wyomin'. They're really powerful, so I have to be careful 'bout who I show them to." He then began moving them around the table, picking up a rather triangular shaped one. "This one here's extra powerful. You can touch 'em, but ya gotta be careful. I don't want anything to happen to ya."

"I'll be careful," I said, as I picked up the crystals. They seemed like plain quartz crystals, with pieces of dirt stained to some of the surfaces. "I'd like to give them to ya, but like I said, they're kinda powerful and I don't know what would happen."

"That's okay, Rodney. You keep them. They're your treasures. But there is something I'd like to give you." I then took off the onenju I was holding and gave it to him.

"Just a moment," he said. He then took his cup of tea and drank all of it, tapping on the bottom to get the tea leaves. Wiping his hands on his pants, he accepted the onenju from me. "Thanks, how do I hold 'em?"

"I hold them in my left hand to remind me of my humanity. There are times when I forget about what I'm here for and they help remind me." He then carefully placed the onenju around his left hand.

"Thanks a lot. There's something I'd like to leave with you, too. I have it in my bag." We then left the kitchen and walked back to the bag he had left in the hallway. He carefully pulled out a rolled-up cloth. Inside the cloth he had a rosary and a strand of what looked like boot laces, wrapped with colored wire and pull tops from cans. On one end was wire wrapped together into a kind of hook. On the other end was wire fashioned in the shape of a cross. "When I was in Denver, I saw this Irish rosary and I tried to copy it. Ya put this hook 'round your thumb when ya hold it." He carefully showed me how to hold his handcrafted rosary. He then placed it on my hand to show me how to hold it.

"Thank you, Rodney, but I think you should keep it for yourself. It obviously means a lot to you."

"No, I want ya to have it."

"Thank you. I'll take good care of it."

He kind of smiled and said, "Well, thanks for the tea and beads. I gotta be going."

"Will you be all right? Do you have a place to stay?"

"I'll be fine, thanks." He picked up his bag and put on his layers of clothes and gloves. He then carefully placed the onenju on his left hand. We shook hands and as he walked toward the door, he dropped a little red cloth heart-shaped coin purse. "Rodney, you dropped your heart," I said handing it to him.

"Nah, you keep it, okay? That thing's been givin' me nothin' but grief." He then walked out the door. I watched as he adjusted his clothes and walked off down the street.

I keep the rosary and the heart that Rodney left with me that day. I learned a lot from Rodney from our short time together. Maybe instead of my answering any questions or helping him find a path of some sorts, it was Rodney that left me with much more than I could have given him.

As I write this article, I look at the heart Rodney left with me. "Living the truth in your heart without compromise brings kindness into the world. Attempts at kindness that compromise your heart cause only sadness." Although an anonymous monk from the 18th century wrote this passage, I realize that the only way to live the truth in my heart without compromise is to trust in Amida Buddha, for with the realization that Amida Buddha takes care of me, just as I am, my ordinary heart can be transformed to the heart of true kindness and compassion.

However, compromise to my heart comes with my own calculation. I'm sure Rodney and all the rest of us have been filled with grief and sadness because of our defiled hearts. It is only through the understanding of True Compassion, Amida Buddha's compassion, that we can bring kindness into the world.

As a result of our own defiled hearts we think, "I'm right; others are wrong. I know better than everyone else." When things don't go our way, we attack those that don't agree with us. It is our defiled, self-centered minds that bring grief into the world. I think Rodney may understand this better than many of us. As I have come to this temple, I have met many interesting people. Rodney had nothing materially, yet he was willing to give what little he had. He understood that it was his heart that brings him grief. I hope that Rodney can be without grief, for even a short time, by leaving his heart at the temple.

"Heretical views caused by ignorance flourish; they grow into forests of bramble that entangle defiled hearts. This causes individuals to be suspicious and slanderous of those with faith in Nembutsu; hence violent attacks by people poisoned with anger abound."

I have also learned that you cannot always trust those that come to you with clean smiling faces. For it is often hard to see the human heart and ignorance behind the mask of affluence and smiling faces. I have seen and am aware that there are members of many temples that think they own the temple. The temple is their country club, to be run the way they see fit. Rodney and his ways are much purer and cleaner. Physically they may be clean and seemingly wealthy, but it is the inside that is poor and defiled with greed, anger and ignorance. Maybe we may all learn from Rodney to go beyond our selfishness, anger and ignorance—to leave our defiled hearts to Amida Buddha. When his heart becomes one with ours, we can hear Amida's voice. I believe Rodney's heart is now with Amida Buddha. Where is yours?

The Land of Bright and Light

◆ ◆ ◆

Vow 3. *If, when I obtain Buddhahood, humans and devas in my land should not all be the color of pure gold, may I not obtain perfect enlightenment.*

Vow 4. *If, when I obtain Buddhahood, humans and devas in my land should not all be of one appearance, and should there be any difference in beauty, may I not attain perfect enlightenment.*

Vows 3 and 4 of the 48 Vows of Amida Buddha

Once upon a time there was a land that wasn't very bright or light. In this land lived families of various colors: the red family, yellow family, and blue family. The families basically kept to themselves. The red families stayed among other red families, the yellow families only with other yellows, and the blues with the blues. As a result, the land stayed rather dim and not very bright or light.

For generations these families of color stayed separate and lived only among their own kind. As a result, in each of these separate families of color, beautiful stories, histories and traditions developed. The reds told of how they came from fire. The blues told of how their wonderful blueness came from the sky. The yellows told of their ancestors—the sun and stars. Each of these families would look toward the heavens and remember their ancestors and hope to reach greatness in their own way.

However, the children often wondered why they couldn't play with one another. They would see the other colors playing in the distance and wonder what they were doing. The little reds would go home and ask, "Why can't we play with the other children?" The elder reds would explain, "We have never mixed with the other colors. Our family has a wonderful tradition of redness. Why would you want to leave and become yellow or blue? We think it best that you stay with us reds. You should be proud of who and what you are."

The blue children would go home and ask, "Why can't we play with the reds?" The elder blues would explain, "What a silly question! It's because those other children aren't blue. Doesn't that seem logical? This world has many colors. If we mixed up, how would you know what you are? Blues should stay with blues, reds with reds, and yellows with yellows. Otherwise, all we would get is a bunch of mixed up colors. The world would become black and dark. There would be no order."

The blue children asked, "Is there something wrong with mixed-up colors? Have you ever seen mixed up colors?" The elder blues looked at one another and smiled. "You know, when we were young, we often thought of mixing the colors, just as you do. But we eventually realized that blues should stay with the blues. After all, isn't the sky blue? We should tolerate the other colors, and we do by providing them with the sky. Look into the heavens. Isn't it blue? If the yellows or reds don't like our sky, they could leave. Since they stay, they must like it the way it is. We think it best that you stay with your own kind. It was good enough for me; it was good enough for my grandfather and his mother before him. Enough of this silly talk."

The yellow children would ask their parents, "Father yellow, Mother yellow, why must we remain apart from the other children?" The elder yellows would reply, "Children, we love you for who you are. Our ancestors the sun and the stars shine for all. We came from the sun and stars. We shine on all. However, while shining upon all, isn't the sky still the sky, the sun still the sun and the fire still fire? This is the way of the world: the blues with the blues, the yellows with the yellows, and the reds with the reds. Now go to sleep, my children, and rest."

Time slowly passed in this land not very bright or light. At about the same time, within each of these families, a very special child was born. Each of these children listened to the stories of his or her family histories and loved them. However, questions arose within each of them. The red child began to wonder, "When I walk in the sun, I feel the same warmth as that of my ancestor the fire. I wonder what that means?" The blue child wondered, "I can see the sky and it is vast and beautiful. However, if the sun were not out, would I be able to see the blue?" The yellow child wondered, "The sun provides for all of us; it is warm like fire. With the sun and fire, I can see the blue sky. Isn't it all a part of the same thing?" These questions persisted within each child, and one day the children left their families to find the answer to their questions.

The children, missing their families, walked and walked. Without their knowing it, they were all walking in the same direction from different points. As they neared one another, they each experienced something miraculous. This land that wasn't very bright or light began to change. They saw upon each of their horizons lightness and brightness. From these different points, they began to run towards the light. As the little red, blue and yellow children ran, they suddenly ran into one another.

Great fear filled each of them, for the stories of the mixed colors had been taught well and each had listened. Yet at that same moment of great fear, a great energy burst forth. They each joined one another and began to sail across the sky, red with blue, blue with yellow, yellow with red. Across the land of not bright or light, a wondrously bright and light rainbow filled the sky. Upon each of their families this great and wondrous white light, a mixing of the colors, brought joy and happiness. A rainbow of light filled the world, awakening the families of red, yellow and blue.

Once upon a time there was a land not very bright or light. Yet, through the questions of three children, a wondrous joining of colors began. This is the story of our land of bright and light. To the great joy of the families of red, yellow and blue, it was not blackness that was created, and the colors did not need to mix into nothingness. Rather, through the joining of the hands of the children of color, great light filled the land. These were the new stories that filled the lives of the families in the land of bright and light.

Shelby and Hillel

◆ ◆ ◆

I am a link in Amida's golden chain of love that stretches
around the world.
I will keep my link bright and strong.
I will be kind and gentle to every living thing and protect
all who are weaker than myself.
I will think pure and beautiful thoughts, say pure and
beautiful words, and do pure and beautiful deeds.
May every link in Amida's golden chain of love be bright
and strong, and may we all attain perfect peace.

Dharma school service book

We are living in an age when many people are questioning the values of the society we live in. It is the age-old quest for meaning and significance in one's life. There are thousands of self-help books touting significant breakthroughs in finding this meaning and significance. Some are better than others. One of my favorites has been *Man's Search for Meaning* by Dr. Victor Frankl. As Dr. Frankl writes:

> Modern men and women are caught in an existential vacuum, the total and ultimate meaninglessness of their lives. They lack the awareness of a meaning worth living for. They are haunted by the experience of their inner emptiness, a void within themselves. The existential vacuum is a widespread phenomenon of the 20th century.... No instinct tells them what they have to do, and no tradition tells them what they ought to do; soon they will not know what they want to do.

Within the literature of our age, this condition has often been alluded to. The Russian novelist Fyodor Dostoyevsky writes, "Without a firm idea of himself and the purpose of his life, man cannot live, and would sooner destroy himself than remain on earth, even if he was surrounded with bread."

98

Albert Camus, the noted existentialist writer, observes, "To lose one's life is a little thing and I shall have the courage to do so if it is necessary; but to see the meaning of this life dissipated, to see our reason for existing disappear, that is what is unbearable. One cannot live without meaning."

This hopelessness seems to have come to a head within our country over the past few months. In Littleton, Colorado, two students who had lost or possibly never found the meaning to their lives, gunned down 15 fellow students. As I write this article I have heard that six high school students in Georgia were shot and injured by a fellow student.

Our children are killing one another. This is the most virulent strain of hopelessness in our society today. However, the antidote for this sickness has been around for thousands of years. It is the teachings of the Buddha. There are many who may think Buddhism is too difficult or academic to apply to their everyday lives. Yes, Buddhism can be difficult and academic. However, this is not the essence of Buddhism.

I have often searched for a Buddhist story concerning this criticism. I know of a wonderful story that would hold true for Buddhism, although it is a Jewish story. "It happened that a certain heathen came before Shammai (he and Hillel were the two leading rabbis of their age) and said to him, "Convert me to Judaism on condition that you teach me the whole Torah while I stand on one foot." Shammai chased him away with the builder's rod in his hand. When he came before Hillel, Hillel converted him and said, "What is hateful to you, do not do to your neighbor. This is the whole Torah. The rest is commentary. Now go and study." (*Babylonian Talmud*, Shabbat 31a)

I love this story. If we could all understand this ideal set forth by Hillel and use this as the meaning for our life, we wouldn't have to worry about the significance of life, for it would be obvious from our everyday living where the significance lies.

Within our Dharma school, ever since I was a student, we would recite the Golden Chain. It's been rewritten a number of times. However, the essential meaning has remained unchanged. The version I began this article with is the version we recite in our Dharma school. We adults often forget lessons that are right under our noses. However, these lessons can be the cornerstones for building a sense of meaning in the lives of our children.

For example, the other day my niece Shelby and I were talking. I was teasing her about being the boss of her preschool class. She said, "Uncle Jerry, you're the boss at church, aren't you?" I started to explain that I wasn't the boss, but as the minister of the temple, I am one of her teachers. For a moment her eyes wandered around the room as I rambled on. It was soon obvious she wasn't interested in learning about the hierarchy of the temple leadership. She politely let me finish my explanation of where I stood as the minister of the temple. As soon as I stopped talking, she went on, "Well, that's nice, Uncle Jerry, but I told my teacher at school you were the boss. As the boss of the church you tell us what to do." I shook my head as she continued on, "And I told her you teach us things. I told her you always teach us to be kind and gentle to every living thing. Isn't that right?"

I was so proud of what she said; there wasn't much else I could tell her. All I replied was, "Yes, Shelby, to be kind and gentle to every living thing is what we learn at Dharma school. Namo Amida Butsu is Amida Buddha telling us to be kind and gentle to every living thing. You know, like our Golden Chain." With that she began to say parts of the Golden Chain.

As a minister and uncle, this conversation with Shelby was as wonderful as when I first read the story of Hillel. Hillel is considered one of the greatest leaders within Jewish history. Shelby is my five-year-old niece. I prefer Shelby's story as an example of the simplicity and beauty of the Buddha's teaching. As I said before, I had searched for a Buddhist story such as the discourse between the heathen and Hillel. Now I had a Buddhist story just as strong from Shelby, the Boss of the Bountiful Kindercare Preschool.

In an age when hopelessness seems the norm, when others are searching for a meaning and significance in their lives, let us not forget to remember the lessons of our youth, such as the one to be found in the Golden Chain. If we can offer this to our children in efforts to bring meaning to their lives, how can their lives not be filled with significance? More than material wealth, it is within the Three Treasures of the Buddha, Dharma and Sangha that our children and we can find the true richness in our lives. I hope you will continue to teach yourselves and your children well. It can be as simple as Namo Amida Butsu.

Another Ghost Story

The Buddha's power is without limits, and so even one who is heavily laden with the hindrances of karmic evil is not burdened. The Buddha's wisdom is without bounds, and so even one who is bewildered and wayward is never abandoned. Only faith is of supreme importance, and nothing else is necessary.

Shinran Shonin, *Yuishinsho-mon'i (Notes on the Essentials of Faith Alone)*

What scares you? How do you answer when someone shouts "Boo!"? I love scary movies and television shows. This is the time of year when there are ghost stories and various scary movies on every night. In one magazine I read about the increase in exorcisms around the country. They asked the question, "When should you call for an exorcist?" The answer was, "When a person close to you begins to change: begins to have an aversion to holy things, speaks in foreign languages that they have never studied and exhibits super-human strength."

I had to laugh to myself when I read that. I don't think I would stick around too long if my five-feet-tall Filipina wife, Carmela, started singing in German, and picked up the sofa over her head shouting, "Get away from me, priest!" I may have to start taking some new medication; I don't know about an exorcist though.

I still remember when the movie *The Exorcist* came out. Many of my friends were terrified of this movie. My friend's younger sister went to a drive-in theater with some friends to see it. A couple of high school boys and these girls thought they would be brave enough to watch this movie. This seemed like the perfect setting for some fun, so my friends and I thought we would just so happen to go to the same movie. We spotted their car and in the middle of the movie, and during one of the scarier scenes, I tossed a Ouija board into the car to see what would happen. The boys screamed louder than the girls. If I remember correctly, the boys jumped out of the car, leaving their dates behind.

There is something about scary things that I just enjoy. Carmela hates them, and I have tried to explain to her there is nothing to be afraid of. She thinks it might be a remnant of her Catholic upbringing. I explained that since she is now a Buddhist, she doesn't have anything to worry about. From a Catholic standpoint, she is already fallen in with the devil. She's destined for hell anyway, so why would the devil risk scaring her into becoming Catholic again? It's like having a large spiritual warning sign on your head from the devil to all demons or ghosts. "Stay away from this one, she's mine or else; she's mine! Signed, The Devil." From a Buddhist standpoint, it is her mind that is causing her to be afraid. What the mind creates, the mind controls. However, she tells me that the fear isn't rational; it just is.

I have tried to convince her how as a Buddhist she shouldn't fear such superstitious things. However, I remember the time I met a ghost in my house about five years ago. It was late at night and everyone in the house was asleep. This is the time I would relax and enjoy watching anything I wanted—no Disney Channel or Nick at Night. This particular night I was watching some special about haunted hotels or something like that. All the lights were out except for the television.

I was sprawled out on the sofa when I heard a creaking sound. At first I thought it must be one of the dogs wandering around. However, the noise kept up and I had to look up to see what it was. To my surprise, the recliner was rocking back and forth on its own. I assumed one of the dogs had bumped it, so I continued watching, waiting for it to stop. To my amazement, it didn't slow down or stop. It began to rock a little faster. As I watched in amazement, in my head I could hear the little girl from the movie *Poltergeist* telling me, "They're here!"

I jumped up and turned on the lights, staring at the chair rocking back and forth on its own. I called for my dogs, "Sammy! Shoyu!" They both came to me sleepily, not from behind the chair, as I had hoped, but from the other side of the room. The little boy from the movie *The Sixth Sense* suddenly flashed into my mind, saying, "I see dead people." Yes, I now knew what he was talking about. I was now saying to myself, "Jerry, be reasonable. Chairs do not rock on their own." I quickly went though all the possible explanations: "Dogs, no, earthquake, no," etc.

My heart was pounding, and just as I was about to scream and wake everybody up to witness our haunted chair, I spotted the demon. She was hunched in the dark corner behind the chair, rocking it back and forth. She spoke in a whispered voice, "Daddy, did I scare you? I can't sleep." It was Kacie, my daughter. She herself seemed a little frightened, probably from the look of panic on my face. I let out a sigh of relief, picked her up, and we both had a good laugh.

This taught me that no matter what we may say or how resolute we are in our opinions about some things, in reality, you just never know. As I have preached to others about not being superstitious, the manipulations of a child had me changing my opinion pretty quickly, believing in the devil's minions. As a result, I know that spiritually, all I can do is rely on Amida Buddha. The answer to "Boo!" is "Namo Amida Butsu."

The Terror Within

◆ ◆ ◆

Let us cease from wrath and refrain from angry looks. Nor let us be resentful when others differ from us. For all men have hearts, and each heart has its own leanings. Their right is our wrong, and our right is their wrong. We are not unquestionably sages, nor are they unquestionably fools. Both of us are simply ordinary people. How can anyone lay down a rule by which to distinguish right from wrong? For we are all, one with another, wise and foolish like a ring, which has no end.

Shotoku Taishi

The events of Tuesday, September 11th, have affected and will continue to affect and change each of our lives and the way we live. The deaths and injuries, both physical and mental, were horrendous, and each of us has been changed forever by what has happened. And just as the death of a family member causes many of us to react with anger, disbelief, sadness and grief, death nonetheless teaches us about the ever-changing nature of life. No matter how much we may try to understand the fact that death is a part of living, when it comes and touches us, we tend to react in surprising ways.

Something that surprised me was my own anger and feelings of revenge and retribution in light of the terrorist acts. Along with many others in our country, I felt we should swiftly find and bomb the country and individuals that carried out this horrendous crime. However, as the day wore on and the news media continued to say that this was like Pearl Harbor, I realized that this was the same type of hysteria that led to the incarceration of Japanese Americans at the onset of World War II. Such is the nature of those of us living in ignorance. Anger and hatred are often just below the surface.

The nature of us human beings is often to strike out first before thinking of the cause of our anger and the ramifications for our actions. We want to blame others for traits and instincts that are within each of us. As we heard the news of this terrifying and horrendous atrocity, we wanted to blame someone or something. I was also appalled when I heard that some members of a Christian televangelists' group had blamed this act on God's lifting his veil of protection from the United States as a result of its support of gays, feminists, abortion and the ACLU. This hatred and religious intolerance obviously is not something that is solely a trait of the Taliban or the followers of Osama bin Laden. It is within each of us.

However, during times of crisis, there is a need within us to do something. The tremendous outpouring of compassion that swiftly spread throughout the country and entire world moved me deeply. Although as a Buddhist I do not sing "God Bless America" or such songs invoking God's blessings or protection for our country, I fully understood the feelings that prompted them. We are Buddhists living in a very Christian-oriented society and as a result must understand Christian beliefs and feelings.

As my daughter Kacie walked through the house singing "America the Beautiful," I sang along with her. As she practiced her Pledge of Allegiance, I recited it with her. I did not tell her, "As Buddhists we don't say 'one nation under God.'" There is a time and place for this type of lesson and this was not the place. Yet, I tried to explain to her that, especially at times like this, we need to try to follow the Buddha's teaching of love and compassion for all beings. This is an act that we can take part in, to love one another to the full extent of our abilities. During these times it is our responsibility to help others.

This is what we can do: act with love and kindness to one another. If we understand the laws of karma, then Tuesday's act of terrorism is a good example. There were eighteen or nineteen hijackers that carried out the destruction that has hurt so many millions of people. Isn't it amazing what a few people can do to change the world? These men, with hatred and anger filling their hearts, managed to hurt so many people. Imagine if, rather than acting out in revenge, anger and hatred, we moved with acts of cooperation, love and kindness in our hearts. We could change the world with love to negate the karma of hate.

The passage I began this essay with is from Shotoku Taishi, the founder of Japanese Buddhism. As he said, "Let us cease from wrath

105

and refrain from angry looks. Nor let us be resentful when others differ from us. For all men have hearts, and each heart has its own leanings. Their right is our wrong, and our right is their wrong." It is not for us to judge others. As an example, it was religious hatred and intolerance that have created this terrible tragedy. These were the feelings of the terrorists—that what they did was for their religion.

In the United States, I have mentioned that some religious leaders are saying that the tragedy of 9-11 is proof that God has abandoned his protection of the United States because of our liberal thinking on abortion and gay rights. Are any of these thoughts sensible? The seeds of hatred are within each of us, Americans and Taliban; all we can do is try to work on ourselves to try not to hate, to try to love all sentient beings. This is something we can do. This is what we should each dedicate ourselves to.

As adults, we should rein in our anger and work with love and compassion. For many of our Dharma school students, they can begin by being nice to all the people in their classrooms and neighborhood—not just their friends, but everyone. If eighteen men filled with hatred could change the world with terror, imagine what all of us could do, moving with love and kindness. This is the heart of the Buddha's teaching of love and compassion. As our Christian friends sing "God Bless America," let us realize that Amida Buddha's loving compassion blesses each and every one of us throughout the universe. We can help funnel this compassion with our actions. As the *Dhammapada* states, "Let us live happily then, hating none while in the midst of men who hate. Let us dwell free from hate while among men who hate." Namo Amida Butsu.

Horace the Hoonko Hippo

◆ ◆ ◆

One day while I was reading the *Letters of Rennyo (Gobunsho)*, I began to feel very sleepy. This isn't uncommon when I am studying and reading passages that require a great deal of thinking. However, suddenly I noticed a Post Script in the letters that I had never noticed before. It was in one of Rennyo's letters about Hoonko. It read as follows:

PS

On the eve of the founder's memorial service the great Hoonko Hippo, Horace, will rise up from the depths of the jeweled ponds of the Pure Land to shout Namo Amida Butsu, as a reminder to all the children of Nembutsu followers that they are embraced by Amida Buddha, never to be abandoned. Thus, this passage may also be known as Hoonko Hippo no sho. (The Letter on the Hoonko Hippo)

Listen to these words; listen to these words…

The Story of Horace the Hoonko Hippo.

In the deepest, darkest reaches of Africa lived a rather grouchy Hippo named Horace. Horace was just dissatisfied with his lot in life. He didn't like having to live in the river all the time. It really affected the reception on his television. He really liked the Animal Planet station but was extremely jealous of the elephant and the white rhinoceros because of how wonderful these programs made them out to be. They were big like him, yet they didn't have to live in the river. He was also jealous of the whale, his other cousin, for the whale was big but had the entire ocean to swim in. Horace wasn't happy with anything about his life. On Christmas, he also didn't get everything he thought he needed.

Well, one day as Horace was thinking all these negative thoughts, he popped his head out of the river and guess whom he saw. It was Santa Claus. He was watering Rudolph and the rest of the reindeer after a practice run around the world. Santa noticed Horace and naturally shouted out with glee, "Ho Ho Ho, Horace, Merry Christmas!"

When Horace heard this he shouted back, "What do I have to be merry about? And besides, Christmas was just over with and you didn't bring me that toy I wanted. Is that why you are here? If not, you are either way early or late." Santa just smiled at Horace and walked over and patted him on the head. Horace continued his complaints, "You know, Santa, besides you letting me down, I don't get any respect from the world. I can run nineteen miles per hour, but have you ever heard anyone say, 'As swift as a Hippo?' I don't think so. On these nature programs you always hear about the majestic elephant or the rare and wondrous white rhinoceros. I've never been called majestic or rare and wonderful. They always just show me yawning and hanging out in the river."

Santa smiled and then suddenly said, "Horace, I have a job for you! You know there was a time when my lead reindeer, Rudolph, didn't get to play in any reindeer games. He was treated as a freak because of his big red nose, but look at him now. He is the most famous reindeer of all. Each of us is special and has a purpose in life. Horace, in life you are embraced by the river, just as you are. The river doesn't ask anything of you, even though you may complain and wish you didn't have to live in it. The river continues to support you and accepts you just as you are.

"We all have a place in this world, and just as you are embraced by the river, all sentient beings are embraced in Amida's compassion. So, Horace, with your mouth so wide, won't you teach all the children about Amida Buddha's compassion and the Nembutsu? And the reason you didn't get that one toy you saw in the commercial is that you haven't been the nicest hippo, have you? And do you really need a *fushigi* ball? You don't even have fingers."

Horace suddenly began bellowing "Namo Amida Butsu. Namo Amida Butsu. I get it, I get it!" And as he did this, he rose slowly into the air, as light as a feather. Santa then led Horace to the jeweled ponds in the Pure Land where Horace now lives. It has been written that on Hoonko Eve, he rises up out of the jeweled ponds, shouting out the Nembutsu to remind us of all we have to be grateful for. Some have even said that on Hoonko Eve, Horace the Hoonko Hippo visits certain good girls and boys who have been especially grateful. He gives them all the things they saw in television commercials during the Christmas season and needed but didn't get. So if you are reading this and didn't get all that you wanted, it means that you have all that you need. Let's join Horace in spreading the word: Happy Hoonko! Namo Amida Butsu!

Gay Buddhist Marriage

◆ ◆ ◆

To undertake the training to avoid taking the life of beings.
To undertake the training to avoid taking things not given.
To undertake the training to avoid sensual misconduct.
To undertake the training to refrain from false speech.
To undertake the training to abstain from substances which
*   cause intoxication and heedlessness.*

The Five Precepts

The deed that causes remorse afterwards and results in weeping and tears is ill done. The deed that causes no remorse afterwards and results in joy and happiness is well done.

Dhammapada

There seems to be a great controversy about the legalization or recognition of gay marriages in this country. I have been asked by a number of people what the Buddhist viewpoint is in regards to this subject. The

109

area that this subject would fall under is Buddhist ethics and morality. This is a very large and convoluted area of research, so I would like to simplify the subject by explaining it through my own simplistic understanding of Buddhist ethics and morality.

In Buddhism, the actions that we create are based on body, speech and thought. Each of these types of actions has consequences. If you hit someone, it may result in your getting beat up, another person's getting hurt, your being thrown in jail or out of school, or possibly all three. If you say something good or bad about someone, there are obvious consequences. If you hate someone, the consequences are that you will be extremely stressed and the hate will probably create problems that will eventually engulf your own life and cause you more suffering than the object of your hate.

From a Buddhist ethical standpoint, when you are making a choice about the actions you commit, you should first ascertain whether that action will be harmful to yourself or to others. If you are working toward acting in a Buddhistic manner, the choice of action would be to avoid harmful actions. As the Buddha said in the *Dhammapada*, "The deed that causes remorse afterwards and results in weeping and tears is ill-done. The deed that causes no remorse afterwards and results in joy and happiness is well done." This practice results in the development of a skillful way of thinking. Sometimes we call this mindfulness.

As for moral conduct, the basics for our lay-centered lifestyle would be based upon the five precepts. These five precepts are very different from the Christian Ten Commandments. With the Ten Commandments, a breach of a particular commandment can result in punishment by God. In the case of the five precepts, a breach would result in negative consequence and one should be aware of the consequence and try to avoid it in the future. As to negative consequence, this would pertain to the question of whether the result had caused harm to oneself or others.

I would say that the Buddhist response to the breach of a precept would result in fewer feelings of guilt than the Judeo-Christian equivalent. Buddhism places a great emphasis on training of the mind to cultivate a calm and peaceful lifestyle and in the process, avoid the mental anguish associated with remorse, anxiety, guilt, etc. This cultivation of a peaceful lifestyle is done through trying to follow the five precepts.

The first precept is to avoid taking the life of beings. This precept refers to all beings and living things and is not limited to humans. Therefore, some people have used this precept as the rationale for their choice of vegetarianism. My personal feeling in this regard is that my living results in the death of countless living beings. Whether I eat meat or vegetables, I have killed. This same question can be taken to the subject of abortion or service in the military, both of which result in death. Abortion results in the death of a fetus. In the majority of cases, the military results in the death of someone.

Buddhism does not make the decision for you. Yet it encourages you to be mindful of your actions and the consequences. For me, mindfulness is in understanding the gratitude I have for life. As to food intake, I should be aware of the lives sacrificed for my living and express gratitude. In the case of abortion, I do not know what the consequences would be for the mother or father of the unborn child, so I could not make a judgment. It is *their* personal choice. As for the military, I would hope that there is no war, but I am grateful that there are other human beings that are in the military to protect my family, my country and me.

The second precept of not taking things not given is a pretty obvious statement. Yet how often have you taken time out from your job in the way of taking a few extra minutes for your lunch hour or being late for school or work? If you are paid six dollars an hour, that roughly breaks down to ten cents a minute. If you were ten minutes late, you have taken one dollar from your employer. If you make more than six dollars an hour, you do the math. This precept is not just about stealing money. It can also refer to taking credit for something you didn't do, but were rewarded for. I think that most of us have broken this precept.

The third precept of avoiding sensual misconduct is where the question of gay marriage would fall. In Buddhism, there is no basic difference between homosexuality and heterosexuality.

In Pali, the actual precept says, *Kamesu micchacara veramani sikkha-padam samadiyami*. The literal translation of this precept is "I take the rule of training not to go the wrong way for sexual pleasure." There are some that may also translate it as sensual rather than sexual. If we were to do this, we would also have to take in the sensual aspect of food, or in the Christian vernacular, the sin of gluttony. In doing wrong or caus-ing harm to oneself or others, what harm is done in eating a large juicy bacon cheeseburger, along with a large order of fries and diet cola? This is the view that a Buddhist should take. Living in a largely Christian society, it is so easy for some of us to act as though our own religion follows similar morals and to judge others accordingly. But as Rev. Mas Kodani said, "I hopefully live in a Christian, Muslim, Jewish, Hindu and Buddhist society."

One of the Christian arguments against homosexuality is that it goes against nature. There have been countless studies showing that ho-mosexuality is natural for the homosexual individual. Homosexuality is a natural response for some human beings and animals, just as het-erosexuality is for others. If we agree that sexuality is a natural part of the human psyche, we must ask what is natural about celibacy, which is encouraged by the Catholic priesthood.

Another argument is that it is written in the Bible that homosexu-ality is condemned. If you were to read the Bible closely, it also ar-gues that women should be socially isolated during menstruation, that working on the Sabbath in some instances should result in capital pun-ishment, and that parents should kill their children if they worship any god other than the Christian God. I believe and hope that there are few Christians who believe in following these ideas even though they are in the Bible. Yet homosexuality is condemned simply because the Bible says so. If we were to use the Buddha's words from the *Dhammapada* to judge homosexuality, or in this instance homosexual marriage, the deed which causes remorse afterwards and results in weeping and tears is ill done. The deed that causes no remorse afterwards and results in joy and happiness is well done. What do you believe to be the result? I have observed only tears of joy from those couples that were finally recognized as a couple. Why would you deny them that because of your own personal prejudice or discrimination?

The fourth precept is to refrain from false speech. Although lying is the obvious action, gossip, rumor and other talk that leads to weeping and tears would also be a breach. Have you gossiped lately?

The fifth precept is to abstain from substances that cause intoxication and heedlessness. Although some people have used this as an argument against drinking, this precept is in a special category and is not imposing evil upon intoxicating substances. Rather, it is a warning that indulging in these substances may result in breaching the other four precepts. As you may see, morality and ethics in Buddhism are to be judged from a different perspective from that of our Christian friends.

For myself, I have found that I have broken each of these five precepts many times. I try not to break them, but I am weak. As Shinran says, "Immeasurable is the light of Wisdom. Of all beings with limited attributes, none are unblessed by the Light. Take refuge in true illumination." With my limited attributes I can only try to be mindful of my actions and to try to act without causing harm to others and myself. I really don't have time to be judging others while trying to be mindful of my own actions. I am grateful that Amida Buddha accepts me as I am. This doesn't mean that I can or will do that for others or myself, but only that I will try. As a result, all I can do is to deeply respond with a grateful Namo Amida Butsu.

I have found a lot of information in regards to this subject on the website buddhanet.net. I would encourage you to look there for a wide variety of information pertaining to Buddhism.

Immigration Within the Six Realms

♦ ♦ ♦

Give me your tired, your poor,
Your huddled masses yearning to breathe free,
The wretched refuse of your teeming shore;
Send these, the homeless, tempest-tost to me,
I lift my lamp beside the golden door.

Emma Lazarus, "The New Colossus"

In Buddhism we divide the world we live in into six realms (*rokudo*). These realms are hell (*jigoku*), hungry ghosts (*gaki*), beasts (*chikusho),* fighting demons (*ashura),* human beings (*ningen*) and heavenly beings (*tenjin*). In our everyday life we move from realm to realm. Our goal is to try to live within the realm of human beings, for it is only within this realm that enlightenment is possible.

In the lower realms of existence we cannot gain enlightenment because of the constant suffering we are in. It drives us beyond the ability to even imagine an escape. Our lives are controlled by instincts alone. It is a world without empathy, altruism or even the ability for self-reflection. It is a world of self-entitlement. Happiness will never be found in this world. Buddhism teaches us that happiness can only be found by giving to others. In these realms we live by the motto "What do I need and want?" and not "What may I do for others?"

In the realm of heavenly beings, enlightenment is also not possible. Within this realm, pleasure is the goal. There is a difference between pleasure and happiness. Pleasure is like traveling to Japan in business class on Japan Airlines. For the thirteen-hour flight you are kept as comfortable as possible. When you want something to drink, you ring a bell and it is brought to you. When you are hungry, you ring a bell and they bring it to you. For entertainment you have a video screen in front of you. However, when that flight ends and your next flight is not in business class, all you can think of is how to get back to business class. You have now been transported from the heavenly realm back to the realm of the hungry ghosts, constantly looking for more. While in those cramped seats of economy class, you long for the pleasure of the reclining business class section. It is a vicious cycle between the lower realms and the heavenly realm, back and forth.

My generation, the baby boomers, are now defining much of our public policy. We live in and were born and raised in a society of entitlement. Most of us have never been to war. I remember the Vietnam War, but the draft ended before I was eighteen and I had no interest in joining the military. My father used the army as a threat: If I didn't hurry and graduate from college, he would make me join the army. The Vietnam War was a very unpopular war. Shouldn't all wars be unpopular?

I believe that as a result of the brutal devastation witnessed and experienced by my parents' generation during World War II, their societal consciousness realized how bad any war could be. Those generations wished that their children never experienced the atrocity and fear that war brings out: Gold Star mothers, concentration camps both Nazi and domestic, rationing of basic necessities such as food and gas. Many from this generation were also the children of immigrants. These immigrants came from such countries as Germany, Italy, Greece, Japan, and China to build a better life for their children and the future generations.

Asian families had experienced the various Asian exclusion laws that had tried to limit Asian immigration. There were national laws such as the Chinese Exclusion Act of 1882, the Geary Act of 1892, and the Page Law of 1875. Asian peoples immigrating to the United States at that time were called the Yellow Peril. The popular press often explained how "Orientals" were dirty or less than human. As a result, it was very easy to shuttle off the Japanese Americans, many of whom were U.S. citizens, to concentration camps during World War II.

My generation experienced very few of the hardships my parents' generation had lived through. In comparison, we live in luxury, business, and first-class living accommodations. Life goes in cycles. Have we returned to the lower realms, back to the economy seats of existence?

Once again we are on the verge of World War. Once again we fear immigration. The shrieks of *ashura* (fighting demons) and *gaki* (hungry ghosts) are all around us. Where is the voice of our human spirit?

My dog and cat, Ponzu and Baby, always fight over territory in our house. I can hear Baby hissing and Ponzu growling in the middle of the night. I have to yell at them to stop their fighting. There are times when I have left them alone for the night. When I return in the morning, I can smell cat urine, or Ponzu will have pooped on the carpet. It really makes me mad and I have to tell myself, "They are only animals marking their territory. They can't help it. They don't know any better." Until they can go beyond this type of thinking, I wonder if they will ever attain enlightenment.

Over the past few weeks I have been reading and hearing about immigration reform. Immigrants built our country; the only natives to this land are the Native Americans and they probably came from Asia. When we speak of the glories of the United States and extol our national values, we often bring up the image of the Statue of Liberty. On the base of the Statue of Liberty is a passage from the poem "The New Colossus." I have begun this article with this passage. This is the essence of the experiment in democracy called the United States. Nowhere in this poem are exceptions to race, creed, color or national origins. This is a very human voice.

I have heard the voice of opposition to immigration reform over the news. Men and women speak about how it will take away from what we have as Americans if we allow too much immigration into this country. I heard one woman saying, "Why don't they just go back to where they came from?" As I listen to this type of thinking, in attitude it reminds me of Ponzu and Baby marking their territory. It smells the same and it looks and feels the same; only this time it is coming from the mouths of beings in human form. I wonder about our ability to attain enlightenment. I hope that my children's generation can come back to live in the human realm. It is possible. Let freedom ring. Namo Amida Butsu.

Seeds of Compassion

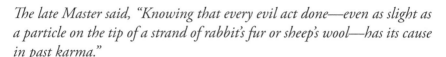

The late Master said, "Knowing that every evil act done—even as slight as a particle on the tip of a strand of rabbit's fur or sheep's wool—has its cause in past karma."

Tannisho, Chapter 13

The tragedy at Virginia Tech is another reminder of how I am capable of violent, selfish acts. Over and over we have been reminded of the possible reasons that Seung Hui Cho committed these heinous acts: bullying, discrimination, mental illness. We have seen how the families of the victims grieve for the loss of their loved ones. It is easy to feel for them in their loss and it is easy to feel anger toward Seung Hui Cho. To look out is an easy response. What may not be so easy is to realize that each of us has the potential for violence within us. It is because I have been the recipient of the compassionate acts of others in my life, that I have not been allowed to release the rage that I have felt.

When I was a boy, there were times that I had been bullied. I can still feel the acidic bile that rises to the top of my throat at being bullied and not being able to do anything about it. I remember that in elementary school I would fight at least once a week. In looking back, I realize that World War II was only 20 years earlier, and the idea of the Japanese as enemy wasn't that far removed from the nation's consciousness. It was "Jap" or "Chink" or some type of ethnic slur that would usually start the fight.

I would have to respond with a challenge to a nearby field after school or immediately react and suffer the consequences from the teacher or principal. Harder than the fighting itself was facing my father with his look of disappointment when he was called to the school and I was kicked out of kindergarten or junior high for fighting. Yet, the fighting was cathartic in that I was able to do something about the bullies or those who called me names. It's different when you can't do anything about the discrimination or hatred directed at you; it burns and festers within your entire being.

I can remember one time when I was being bullied at a Judo tournament in Idaho. The person bullying me was about five or six years older than I was. I must have been about 10 or 11, so this person was about 15 or 16. I had often been teased by this bully and this time I wasn't going to back down. I didn't care if he beat me up, and I was ready to fight him.

I was right next to him and ready to get hit, not expecting anyone to help me. In fact, I was aware of others gathering around to watch me get beat up, so I was surprised when someone spoke up. "Hey, (I won't say his name), what's your problem, picking on him. If you want to fight someone, why don't you fight me? I'm the same size as you, not a little kid like Jerry." Glen Morinaka was about the same age as the bully. Glen was older than I was and not a relative. I didn't really know him.

Glen's confronting the bully changed my life. The bully backed down and left me alone, and for that I am forever grateful to Glen. However, it wasn't just because he saved me from getting beat up, which he did. It was Glen's willingness to see me as a human being and to stick up for someone weaker than himself. This recognition of my hurt and our mutual humanity and his willingness to defend me without really knowing me has instilled within me a sense of compassion for the world.

I have been blessed with this type of karmic seed of compassion throughout my life. I know that without these seeds of compassion I would not be that different from Seung Hui Cho. Although at that Judo tournament Glen saved me from myself, I held a deep hatred for that bully for almost 20 years.

I remember in college I had gotten a lot bigger and it was a rather wild and exciting time in my life. I was quite confident in myself and I thought about finding that bully and physically hurting him, regardless of the consequences. I had worked it out in my mind: where, when, and how I would approach him and take out my vengeance on him. I can still remember seeing the bully for the first time in years. Rather than anger, the feeling that engulfed me was pity. If I had really hurt him as I planned, was he worth my going to prison, the pain my parents would feel, and the loss of my other dreams in life?

The seeds of compassion began to blossom for me, and I realized that there are people in my life that do support and care for me. I began to study Buddhism in earnest from about that time.

If Seung Hui Cho had been as lucky as I to find friends and supporters, if he could see the compassionate embrace of the world in his life, what would his life have been like? If I had not encountered these Bodhisattvas planting the seeds of compassion in my life, where would I be? I could be he; he could be I. Each of us is the recipient of compassion. Some of us are just lucky enough to be shown how to see it. Namo Amida Butsu.

Slot Machine Meditation

◆◆◆

Rivers of blind passions, on entering the ocean—
The great, compassionate Vow
Of unhindered light filling the ten quarters—
Become one in taste with that sea of wisdom.
"Koso Wasan" 43, *CWS,* p. 371

I love to play the slot machines. This summer while I was in Las Vegas, I played a Wizard of Oz slot machine hoping that I would get a bonus. The bonus is an added incentive for playing the slot machines. It is usually a scene from the theme of the slot machine. In this case, the bonus was either Glinda the Good Witch suddenly appearing and giving you wild bars, a trip to the Land of Oz to visit the Wizard, or a big bonus with the Wicked Witch and her flying monkeys changing all kinds of symbols for wilds. I pushed the button again and again, saying to myself, "Come on, Oz! Come on, Glinda baby! Let me see you."

With each and every push I thought the same thing, just waiting for the bonus to come. Out of one hundred pushes, the bonus came out once, maybe twice if I was lucky. When the bonus did come out, I was grateful for a few seconds, and then I heard my mind thinking, "Yay...bonus. Now give me a big bonus; give me a big bonus! Let's see the witch! Come on, Wicked Witch; come on out. Come on! Let me see the wizard. Where are you, Wizard?"

Here I was hoping for a bonus, and when I got a bonus, rather than enjoy the bonus I had received, I changed my goal to a big bonus. Out of ten bonuses, I got a big bonus once. That means out of 1,000 times, I was happy one time. On this particular machine I tried to see the Wizard, and out of a thousand times, I got to see him once. I doubt that Dorothy, the Lion, the Tin Man or the Scarecrow, no matter how brave, smart or heartfelt their intent, would ever have had the persistence I did to see the Wizard.

This made me think about what it is about playing the slot machines that I really enjoy. Is it the money I win? I have never really won any money playing slot machines. I can count on one hand the times I have hit a jackpot of $1,000. If I have been lucky enough to hit that amount, I have probably put that much in already, so my net gain is already in the red. This means that I have never won a penny playing the slot machines. I have lost many times that amount over the hundreds of times I have been to a casino. Sure, there are the slot machines that have the chance to win millions of dollars. I have played them. Or when I am in California, I have bought lottery tickets that had the chance of winning millions of dollars.

Carmela doesn't gamble, and she always asks me, "Why do you continue to do something you are so bad at?" Somewhere in my mind I realize that she is right. It is silly to play the game if I am expecting to win. If I judge my gambling as successful or unsuccessful by how much money I have brought home in my pocket, I doubt that I will ever be in the position to look back and say, "Wow, I'm good at this. I should get a gold medal for slot machine playing." However, I wonder what I will want once I hit the millions: more money? another big bonus? immortality?

I realized how my bonno (greed, anger and ignorance) just seems to take over when I play the slots. I should play the slot machines just to play the slot machines—to sit in a casino, to listen to the exciting sounds around me, to have enough money to enjoy playing the slot machine. I learned that it isn't the bonuses; it is just playing the game.

It seems as though I often live my life the same way I was playing the slot machines—waiting for the bonuses. When I was in elementary school, I couldn't wait until I was in the sixth grade. In the sixth grade I would be at the top level of the school. Once I was in sixth grade, I longed for junior high. When I made it to seventh grade, I realized I was at the bottom of the pecking order and longed to be in ninth grade or high school. In high school I couldn't wait to drive or get into college. At each and every push of the button, there was always something more I wanted.

At this year's Mountain States Conference, our guest speaker was Gregg Krech, founder of the Todo Institute and author of the book *Naikan: Gratitude, Grace and the Japanese Art of Self Reflection.* The name of the newsletter for the Todo Institute is called "Thirty Thousand Days." I asked him why he chose that title. He explained that the average age for a human being is a little over eighty-two years, which is thirty thousand days. In calculating this out, I realize I have passed the halfway mark. If I have had ten or twenty really great days, such as graduations, marriages, births of my children, etc., where would I classify the other 18,000 days I have used so far?

This is what practice means for Jodo Shinshu Buddhists: striving to look at the days beyond the bonuses and seeing them as being truly meaningful and important; to be able to push the buttons; to hold them with gratitude for the unseen causes and conditions that have allowed me to just live (or gamble). Your life, my life is hitting the jackpot. Waking up, listening to my girls laugh or cry, arguing or enjoying a night out with Carmela, I should see every day as the big bonus. Namo Amida Butsu.

Soo Desu Ka? (Is That So?)

◆◆◆

How boundless the sky of Samadhi unfettered.
How transparent the perfect moon-light of
the fourfold Wisdom!
At that moment what do they lack?
As the Truth eternally calm reveals itself to them,
This very earth is the Lotus Land of Purity,
And this body is the body of the Buddha

Song of Meditation by Hakuin Zenji,
from Manual of Zen Buddhism, translated by D. T. Suzuki

This summer has been very busy. When things get hectic in my life, I forget how good my life is. There was a period of about a month, beginning with our Salt Lake Obon to about August 18, when it felt as if I was on a rapidly-moving treadmill and beginning to fall behind. During this time period I had visited twelve cemeteries throughout Utah and Nevada. I performed and spoke at four Hatsubon/Obon services, four funerals, two weddings and a number of memorial services. I went on a bus trip throughout northern California with our Jr. YBA and also on one with our BWA to the Las Vegas Obon. I flew to the Jodo Shinshu Center in Berkeley for three separate meetings and seminars.

After the Fong family hosted the BWA Japan exchange students, Carmela and I hosted them and I thought I would get a slight break, but I had to prepare for two funerals in Honeyville. The Mountain States District Conference is in a week, and I'm still struggling with this month's article. During this time we also moved everything from the main temple building (yes, including the *naijin*) to the west wing building, and I moved the temple office to my home. Along the way I also had a bout with the flu. Whew! It has been quite a summer.

As I was recovering from my flu and having come down with a slight case of self-pity, I began talking with my daughter Taylor. I don't know where it comes from, but Taylor has an extremely deep side to her nature. Out of the blue, she sometimes amazes me with her insights into life, and she has only been alive for ten years. I really hope that I get the chance to see what another twenty or so years will do to her. She was talking to me about her teacher for the new school year. Taylor said that since kindergarten, she has never gotten the teacher that her older sister Kacie has told her would be the best teacher for that particular grade. However, every teacher she has had has been wonderful and she feels very lucky to have been in his or her class.

I asked her how she thinks this happens. She explained that it had to do with her attitude towards the teachers. She admitted that she always has a certain teacher she would like, but she has never gotten one of those teachers. In fact, usually she not only doesn't get the teacher she hopes for, but she also usually gets the teacher that Kacie tells her is the worst teacher in that grade. I asked her if that's the case, why she thought they had turned out to be so good?

She explained that once she finds out who her teacher is, whether or not it is the teacher she wanted, she doesn't think of it as good or bad. She said at least she has a teacher and a good school to go to. If she were to think one way or the other, she could be disappointed either way, so she remains neutral and lets life work itself out. She says it never fails that if she thinks in this way, things usually turn out well. She told me that she has always been happy about how her school year turns out. I was just amazed listening to her rationale and realized how true her explanation was. And maybe this is just how I needed to look at my summer—not good or bad, just the way it was.

One of the most famous of all Japanese Zen masters was a man named Hakuin Zenji. He is considered the father of the modern Japanese Rinzai Zen tradition. There is a story about how on one occasion a young woman in the village gave birth to a child out of wedlock. She told her parents that Hakuin was the father of her baby. This girl's parents were furious and came to him with the baby. They called him all kinds of names and said that he was responsible for the baby and would have to raise it. Hakuin said only, "Is that so?"

I read this story in English and this is the way it was translated.

I can imagine him rubbing his chin, nodding his head and saying, "Ahh…soo desu ka?" which can be translated as "Is that so?" They left the baby and Hakuin gently and lovingly took care of the baby, never complaining. After a few months, the young woman finally confessed that it was not Hakuin, but a young man in the village who was the real father. The girl's parents immediately went to Hakuin, apologized and asked for the baby. Hakuin rubbed his chin and said, "Ahh, soo desu ka?" He went and gave the baby back to the couple.

As we can see from this story, Hakuin had the ability to just see life as life. Allowing our life to flow just as it is and not judge it as good or bad is how we can open ourselves to happiness. One of Hakuin's famous poems is called "Song of Zazen," sometimes called "In Praise of Zen." He writes, 'How boundless the sky of Samadhi unfettered. / How transparent the perfect moon-light of the fourfold Wisdom! / At that moment what do they lack? / As the Truth eternally calm reveals itself to them, / This very earth is the Lotus Land of Purity, / And this body is the body of the Buddha."

From the mouth of my child, I have heard the insight of the great Zen master Hakuin. Maybe I should have called her Taylor Zenji. In retrospect, this has been a very good summer. I became a minister because there was a time when I believed that no other profession would allow me to be a part of the important and transitional times in the lives of others, both happy and sad occasions. There are times when I foolishly forget about how lucky I am. This summer I have truly been blessed to take part in the life of our Sangha. Namo Amida Butsu!

Death

I believe that our own physical death is one of the experiences in life that we can never truly believe or understand. However, death may be our greatest teacher. Whether the death is that of a loved one or the thought and fear of our own, there is no denying its strength in teaching us how we should live. Death comes in many forms. One of the most important Buddhist teachings is the law of impermanence. Change is also a form of death.

Daddy, What Does It Mean to Die?

◆ ◆ ◆

It is hard for us to abandon this old home of pain, where we have been transmigrating for innumerable kalpas down to the present, and we feel no longing for the Pure Land of peace, where we have yet to be born. Truly, how powerful our blind passions are! But though we feel reluctant to part from this world, at the moment our karmic bonds to this Saha world run out and helplessly we die, we shall go to that land.

Tannisho, CWS, p. 666

The other day we took Kacie to the viewing of her uncle, George. It was the first time Kacie had really seen a dead body. We had talked of death before, but this was the first time she had really seen the dead body of someone she knew. I feel that the emotions and images that the experience has left her with will remain with her for the rest of her life.

As we walked up to the family and the open casket of Uncle George, I tried to explain to her that Uncle George had died. She asked, "Daddy what does it mean *to die?*"

I said, "Kacie, we are all dying. From the moment we are born, we begin to die. There isn't anything we can do to keep from dying; it's natural, just like living and playing. Sometime you and I will have to die also."

"What happens when we die?"

"When we die, it's like waking up from a dream. You know what it's like to wake up from a dream, don't you?" She nodded her head. "When we die, we go to the Pure Land."

"Oh," she said, somewhat unsure of what I was talking about.

As we walked up to Uncle George, I carried Kacie in my arms.

Looking down into the casket, she just stared at him. I softly said to her, "See Kacie? There's nothing to be afraid of. Doesn't he look like he's sleeping?"

"Daddy, will Uncle George wake up from his dream?"

"No, honey, we won't see him wake up. To Uncle George we are like the dream. This body is only a part of Uncle George. The real Uncle George is awake with Amida Buddha."

"Oh." She continued to stare at him.

While I was explaining these things to her, someone nearby said, "At that age they ask a lot of questions." I just nodded my head in agreement. Kacie then turned and put her head on my shoulder and we walked over to the seats where all the family members were sitting. I placed Kacie in the chair next to me. She leaned into me and I could feel her crying. I asked her, "What's wrong, honey?"

"Daddy, I don't want Uncle George to die.... I don't want to die."

"Kacie, there's nothing we can do about Uncle George, for he has already died. But I hope that you will live for many, many years. But there is nothing to be afraid of. Death is natural. It happens to us all. Someday I will have to die and I don't want you to be afraid when it happens. You might not be able to see me, but I will always be with you. Okay? When you say, 'Namo Amida Butsu,' we will always be together. Okay, honey?"

She looked at me with tears in her eyes and shook her head and said, "But I don't want to die, Daddy."

"I know, honey. I don't want to die right now either." With that she seemed all right for the moment, although I don't know how long until the next barrage of questions.

Kacie is only four years old. When that person said, "At that age they ask a lot of questions," I felt like responding, "Have you ever asked yourself these same questions?" How would you answer them? We often feel that our children ask a lot of questions. As a minister I often get asked, "How do I explain this to my child?" I have to first answer, "How would you explain this to yourself?" How many of you have asked these same questions? How many of you feel comfortable in answering these questions? I believe that these questions are probably some of the most important questions any of us can ask and should ask.

As I answered Kacie's questions, two quotes came to my mind. One quote was from Honen Shonin, where he says, "While alive, we accumulate the virtues of the Nembutsu. When we die, we will go to the Pure Land. Knowing that in either case this self has nothing to be distressed about, I am not worried about either death or life."

The other quote is the one I began this article with. It is from Chapter 9 of the *Tannisho*. I read the first quote in the translation of Rev. Jitsuen Kakehashi's lecture, which he presented at the BCA centennial, entitled "The Shin Buddhist View of Birth and Death." Rev. David Matsumoto translated and edited the lecture into a booklet published by the BCA Research and Propagation Program in association with IBS and the endowment foundation. It's a wonderful talk subtitled "The Path Transcending Life and Death."

As Rev. Kakehashi says in his lecture, "The transcendence of our samsaric existence of birth and death is a problem that is very difficult to solve. Yet, seriously thinking about and seeking to clarify the meaning of our life and our death is the single most important thing that a human being can do."

I know that from my own experience, it was the death of my grandfather and the questions that arose from seeing his body lying in the casket that was the beginning of my own questions concerning life and death. Why did he die? What happened to him? These questions led me to my present understanding and appreciation for our Jodo Shinshu teachings.

I hope that each of you will feel comfortable in asking questions. There are many members of our temple who are afraid to ask these questions. To be honest, they are not easily answered. However, our teachings do have answers and more questions to add to these very important questions of life and death. Let's ask them of ourselves and then we can provide something for our children. In closing, I would like to leave you with a quote from my friend the late Rev. Russell Hamada:

The Buddha did not create this Universe.
The Buddha did not create you.
The Buddha does not punish your evil deeds.
The Buddha does not reward your good deeds.
The Buddha does not cure your illness.
The Buddha does not protect you from harm,
    make you wise or keep you happy.
What then is the Buddha?
The Pure Land is not simply a romantic story,
    it is the real world.
All that you see and do now is the dream.
A self-centered world created for the appeasement
    of your own greed.
What then is the Pure Land?
Now is the time to ask.
If you would know, you must ask,
    or live and die for no reason at all.

Tofu and Quiet Thunder

◆ ◆ ◆

It was a warm and humid evening when I walked through Bachan's (Grandma's) front door into the organized clutter of her 92 years of life. How many times had I walked through this door and called out, "Hi, Bachan," over the din of her television and VCR which would be playing some Japanese videotape? She would walk out from the kitchen, hold my hand, smile and ask, "*Itsu kaita no?*" ("When did you get home?") I would explain to her that I had just returned home for a short visit, to which she would reply, "*Yokkata na, waza waza ae ni kite, arigatoo ne.*" ("That's so nice. Thank you for taking the time to come and visit.")

We would talk a little—I in my tentative Japanese, she in her broken English and Japanese. If my father were with me during our conversations, she would often look to my father for translations as I spoke. He would repeat in his more familiar voice the same things I had just said. Although I had learned to speak Japanese while I was studying in Japan, Bachan still wasn't used to the fact that one of her grandchildren could speak to her in her native tongue. She was accustomed to looking to my father or Auntie Maxine for help in translating her thoughts to us or translating our thoughts to her, so although I was speaking to her in Japanese, she looked to my father.

After a while of chitchat in this strange manner, she would say, "Hungry *dessho, nanika o tebenai ka*?" ("You must be hungry. Why don't you eat something?") I would usually tell her, "No thank you, Bachan. I just wanted to bring you this *omiyage*." I would then give her *manju* (a Japanese sweet) or something Japanese I had picked up in J-town. She would then reprimand me for bringing her anything, explaining to me that she knows that I'm poor—that ministers are poor—and I shouldn't waste the little money I had on her. My father would then tell her, "It's okay, Bachan, Jerry brought it especially for you, so just accept it." She would then nod her head, thank me, and continue telling me how *mottainai* (wasteful) it was for me to spend money on her.

We would then go into the room with her obutsudan, light the candle and incense, and whatever I had brought her as an omiyage would be placed in the obutsudan. Then we would schant "Juseige,"*oshoko* (burn incense), and return to the living room. Bachan would go to the kitchen and bring back some food she had prepared for me, and when my father wasn't looking, slip some money into my hand, motioning for me not to make a fuss or let my father know. I would try to give the money back, which I knew was either a $20 or $50 bill— whatever she had in her purse. She would give me a stern look and tell me to be quiet and just accept it, just as my father had told her to take my omiyage.

This ritual began after I had told Bachan I was going to be a minister. She was very much against it, not because of the job, but because of the financial hardships. The pattern that followed was, "Bachan, don't worry. I don't need any money. I'm fine." She would then explain how she had known and been friends with many ministers and their families and watched their families suffer because of the lack of money. She knew ministers loved their job, but their families suffered because of it. She would explain how she wanted to help alleviate my suffering as much as she was able. She would express how lucky she was to have such successful grandchildren, but since I was the poorest among them, I needed as much financial help as she could provide.

I knew that on Christmas, New Year's and birthdays, as my other cousins received underwear, pajamas or gifts of food, I would always receive cash in addition to some type of food. My father would tell me, "Just take it and say thank you." I would thank her and tell her I would visit again soon. She would hold my hand, thank me for coming, tell me to take care, and once again tell me how mottainai it was for me to bring her the gift and not to do it anymore. This had been the pattern of my visits home for the past ten years or more. However, as I entered her home on one particular night, I knew things would no longer be the same.

It was obvious the situation had changed, for rather than the sound of the TV, there was a large tank, hissing air as it passed oxygen through the tubes leading into Bachan's bedroom. I knew Bachan would not be coming out to greet me. My reason for coming home that night was not just to drop off omiyage. A few days earlier my father had called me in San Jose, explaining how Bachan had experienced a rather severe heart attack and that the doctor's prognosis was not very good. Although I wanted to be as positive as possible, a part of me knew that I was coming home to say goodbye to Bachan.

Auntie Maxine, my dad's older sister, came out of Bachan's bedroom and welcomed me home. I looked into the bedroom as she came out and there was Bachan lying in bed, smiling at me as warmly as she was able through the oxygen hose she was now connected to. I gave Auntie Maxine the omiyage I had brought and went into Bachan's room. As soon as I went in she tried to sit up in bed. She took my hand and asked, "*Itsu kaita no?*" I told her that I had some vacation time, so I wanted to come home for a short visit. She smiled knowingly and merely replied "*Yokkata na.*" (That's nice.) Both of us knew that today was different from my previous visits and she quietly told me that there were some important matters she wanted us to talk about. For the first time, without pausing to look at my father or Auntie Maxine, she spoke to me directly in Japanese.

I asked her, "*Saki ni, chotto Obutusdan no mae ni omairi shimashoo ka?*" ("Shall we first have a short service before the obutsudan?") She smiled and nodded her head in agreement, asking my father to turn off the oxygen so that the candles and incense could be lit, and together we walked to the obutsudan room. She had Auntie Maxine place some of the manju I had brought her into the obutsudan. We then chanted together, burnt incense and recited the Nembutsu. She thanked me, told me how much better she felt, and walked with me back to her room.

As she settled back in, I said, "Bachan, you look good, but you have to rest and get strong."

She smiled and said, "I'm trying, but I'm not afraid to die."

Trying to be as positive and as strong as I could, I said, "Bachan, we don't want to talk about dying now. I know you're ninety-two years old, but it's still too soon for you to die."

Bachan smiled, looked me square in the eyes, and said, "Even if I were 100 years old, wouldn't you say the same?"

We laughed and I agreed with her, but I said she should hold onto life as long as she could, for our lives are wondrous gifts. She nodded her head and took my hand and said, "I know what you mean, but I just want you to know that I'm not afraid of dying. Even if I were to go to hell, I have no regrets about my life. As human beings we sometimes do things that some may say isn't good or proper, but to live in this world, we do what must be done, whether good or bad. Sometimes we do what we do just to live. I have done things like that in my life and I am ready to suffer any consequences that I may have created for myself."

I explained, "Bachan, I have dedicated my life to the teachings of Jodo Shinshu and to try to understand them with my entire being. Of all the teachings, what I most strongly believe is that Amida Buddha will take care of us when the time comes for us to die. If we give up this problem of our death to Amida, we can focus on what we are doing here and now. Bachan, you must focus on resting and getting better. Neither one of us knows when we will die. So let's not worry about what will happen to us at that time. Let's leave that up to Amida. Okay, Bachan?"

Once again she smiled, squeezed my hand a little tighter, sat up a little and said, "I understand. I just want you to know that I am not afraid. I have many good friends and family in this world. All of you are so kind to me and I am grateful for that. I also have even more good friends and family who have died before me and so there is a continuation of this life into the next. Your mother and *Jichan* (grandfather) are waiting for me, so I am not afraid, only grateful for all that I have had up until this moment. However, there are certain things that I want you to understand about this life and that's what I want to talk with you about."

Bachan then released my hand and settled back and began telling me about an experience she had while she was a young lady living in Los Angeles with her father. "When I was younger, I was very stubborn and set in my ways. I felt that the world was very black and white. My father had been a very skilled carpenter in Japan and had a number of apprentices working under him. However, that time in Japan was not good economically and with the responsibility to care and look after his apprentices, my father eventually spent most of his savings. Faced with a bleak future in our village in Yamaguchi, he decided that for us to survive, we must go to America. Not many people from our village had gone to America. My village wasn't a rich village, but it wasn't a poor one either. Therefore, not very many had felt it necessary to go to America. However, my father felt that he had no other choice. He gave what he had left to his apprentices and we left for San Francisco."

"After arriving in America, my father had a hard time finding work in San Francisco. He heard from some other Japanese that Los Angeles was a place with many jobs, so we took what we had and left for Los Angeles. It was very hard for me when we arrived, not having friends or family here. It was not easy being Japanese and living in America. We didn't stay in San Francisco long enough for me to meet any other Japanese. However, when we arrived in Los Angeles, I began attending the Buddhist temple. There were many other young people from Japan whom I could talk to and socialize with. I enjoyed going there for these friendships I developed.

"On one occasion, as I was sitting in the temple listening to the minister's sermon, a young man came in and sat down right next to me. I thought it was funny for him to sit next to me, for there were other open seats throughout the hondo. He made me feel very uncomfortable sitting so close. I looked at him, wondering why he was sitting so close and then he smiled at me. I didn't like that at all. This man just sitting down next to me with so many other seats available and then smiling at me like that really bothered me.

"I think he wanted to talk with me, but I certainly didn't want to talk with him, so I immediately got up and left. At the time, Rev. Kyogoku's wife must have seen what had happened and called me to come sit by her and talk. Rev. Kyogoku's wife was a very wise lady and she told me something that day that has helped me throughout my life, and I want to pass it down to you so that it may help you, and likewise you may be able to use it to help others.

"Mrs. Kyogoku asked me to sit down, and she explained to me that in this world we must get along with others. She used tofu as an example. She said, 'Tofu is always cut into blocks. It is the nature of tofu to be cut into blocks. No matter how soft tofu is, the nature of tofu is to be square, and in their squareness they can be placed next to other tofu. However, human beings are different from tofu: tofu is meant to be square; a human being is not. A human being must be rounded on the edges to live with others and sit with others. A human being who remains square like tofu cannot survive in this world. We humans must have rounded edges.' This is a lesson that I have tried to remember throughout my life. Tofu is meant to be square, humans are not."

I interrupted her and asked, "Bachan, was that man who sat next to you Jichan?" She kind of chuckled and continued, "No, I never saw that man again. I guess I insulted him by getting up and leaving like I did. However, Rev. and Mrs. Kyogoku later introduced me to your Jichan. Jichan was a little wild and liked to dress up in fancy clothes. He tried to act like a tough guy around Japantown. However, even though he acted like this on the outside, inside he was a kind and very intelligent man. He was very active at the temple. He helped start the Young Men's Buddhist Association in Los Angeles in 1910."

"I guess Mrs. Kyogoku thought that both of us needed to have rounder edges and would complement one another. They introduced us and were our *nakaodo* (go-between) at our wedding. I think you're a lot like Jichan. He always felt that the temple was very important. I guess you are carrying on and continuing what Jichan did in his life. I'm sure he would be very happy and proud of you. But I just wanted to explain to you the lesson I learned from Mrs. Kyogoku. As a result of her story, I had a very good life. I want you to have a good life.

"There is one more experience of mine that I want you to remember and learn from. This is also very important, especially in the work that you do, and it concerns the true nature of compassion. It was a lesson taught to me by your mother. As I said, your Jichan was a bit wild and extravagant about the things he did. Sometimes he would do some very crazy things. Sometimes they were dangerous! I would get mad and yell at him, 'That's dangerous! Stop it or you'll get hurt!' However, when your mother saw Jichan doing something dangerous or crazy, she wouldn't yell at him as I did. She would say, 'Jichan, please stop doing that. I don't want to die yet.' When Jichan heard that, he would stop and think about what she said and what he was doing.

"This was true compassion. Your mother understood that our lives are deeply connected to those around us, especially to those we love. If something were to happen to Jichan, it would be as though it happened to her. If Jichan were hurt, she would feel the pain. If Jichan were to die, a part of her would die. From that moment on, I loved your mother as my true daughter. You know when your mother died, a part of me died also.

"However, I have accepted her death and I think it was because of the bond we had nurtured as mother and daughter. One of the most fulfilling moments of my life happened while your mother was very sick with cancer. The medicine she was taking had made her body so bloated and uncomfortable. It was so painful to see her suffer like that. I wanted to try to help relieve some of the pain and make her more comfortable. I asked her if I could massage her. She smiled and I rested her head in my lap and massaged her shoulders and arms.

"Your mother would thank me over and over, but the only reason I was able to do that for her was that she had allowed me to be close to her as a true mother and not merely a mother-in-law. She allowed me to be her mother. She taught me about true compassion and the interconnectedness of our lives. I was only a mother because she always acted towards me as a true daughter. True Compassion is in this interconnectedness of our lives. I know that your mother and I will be together again; this belief has sustained me and allowed me to live with the sadness of her death—the worst experience of my life.

"However, in looking over my life now, I realize what a very good life I have had, with so many wonderful friends and family. I have no regrets in my life. I just wanted to let you know these things so they may help you. I hope you can understand what I have said to you and maybe it may help others." She then looked into my eyes and held my hand once again, making sure I understood the importance of what she was telling me. I held her hand tight, smiled and said, "I understand, Bachan, and I'll try to not look and be like tofu." She smiled at me, and I continued, "But now is the time for you to rest and get strong. I'll come to see you again tomorrow, okay?"

"You don't have to come tomorrow. I'll be okay. But I just wanted to tell you these things. Thank you so much for coming to see me. I know how busy you are." I don't know where it came from, but she placed a $50 bill in my hand, smiled and said good-bye.

I said thank you and left her so she could rest. I saw Bachan every day for the next four days, but we only exchanged a few words. The last time I saw her alive she just smiled and squeezed my hand. I left Salt Lake to return to San Jose. A week later I received a phone call from my father to inform me that Bachan had died. She had gotten over the pneumonia, which had entered her lungs after the heart attack, but her heart was just too damaged for her to recover. I realize the true nature of our existence is much greater than our physical limitations and being. Bachan's human heart may have stopped beating on May 31, 1992; however, her true heart beats along with mine and embraces me with compassion this very moment.

At Bachan's funeral, as at all Jodo Shinshu funerals, the minister recited this passage from the Sutra on Entering the Level of the Land of Pure Faith:

> Flowing and turning in the Three Worlds of delusion
> And unable to sever the bonds of desire and attachment;
> Discarding them now and entering into the Uncreated,
> Becoming a true being of gratitude and indebtedness.

Bachan has been released from the bonds of desire and attachment. Shinran said that he would come back again and again, like the waves of Waka no Ura Bay. A famous Zen master by the name of Koho Kennichi referred to his return as "quiet thunder." At this moment, the lesson of compassion Bachan shared with me continues to ring in my ears again and again like waves of quiet thunder, as I remain in this ocean of birth and death.

One Hundred Years or Just One Day

◆ ◆ ◆

In attentively contemplating the fleeting nature of life, nothing is more fleeting than our journey through this world. It is as an all too short dream. Has anyone lived for 10,000 years? Life swiftly passes, and how many have lived for even a hundred years?

Rennyo Shonin, "Letter on White Ashes"

This past month we have held the funeral services for two of our senior temple members, Mr. Tadao Ushio and Mr. Takataro Shiba. Mr. Ushio was 98 and Mr. Shiba was 100. It's hard for me to think in terms of living that long, yet my thoughts and daily activities seem to be at odds. I am not even half the age of either of these men, yet I act as though I will live forever.

Then there are days when I find myself feeling very old. I think in terms of, "I'll be almost 60 years old when Taylor graduates from high school. I wonder if I'll make it to see her graduate. I had better try to get in shape. I have to quit smoking, eat right and exercise." I psych myself up to do these things, and then I look outside and think, "It's cloudy and it looks like it might rain. I'll start exercising tomorrow. A chile verde burrito would sure be good for lunch."

Although thoughts such as these occur to me on a weekly basis, I still haven't started on a diet or exercise program or quit smoking. I've probably eaten a couple of pigs' worth of chile verde and smoked how many packs of cigarettes, while thinking of dieting and quitting smoking. Procrastination about large, important matters is very easy. I always have tomorrow to take care of them. At least that is what I assume.

However, what would I do if at my next physical my doctor told me, "Jerry, I have some bad news for you. You were right: you have lung cancer and your weight has basically worn your body out. I'm sorry, but you'll probably be dead within the week"? After staring at the doctor in disbelief and after he and the nurses have helped me off the floor, I would probably go home and lie around in shock for a few more hours.

After that I would start to clean my room and office and tell my family how much I love them and appreciate all they have done for me. Next would be to call some friends and talk with them about what they have meant to me. Since many of my friends are fellow ministers, I would arrange my funeral. If I had some time, I would probably write a bunch of letters to Kacie and Taylor to read as they reached certain milestones in their lives. There are a lot of things I would do if I knew I only had so many days to live. This seems logical; but what is so illogical is that none of us really know how much longer we will live. Yet what are we doing about it?

As Jodo Shinshu Buddhists, once we have understood that Amida Buddha will take care of us, this important matter will free us to focus on a life of gratitude. Yet how many of us are living such a life? All of these things I have listed are things that I could do now. Why don't I? Whether I live only one day or I live one hundred years, what am I doing with the life I have at this moment? I've just said I felt old. I know that I am living a fairly unhealthy lifestyle, and I don't express appreciation for the things that I have. This is what we mean by saying we are all foolish beings.

Shinran writes, "What a joy it is that I place my mind in the soil of the Buddha's Universal Vow and I let my thoughts flow into the sea of the Inconceivable Dharma! I deeply acknowledge the Tathagata's Compassion and sincerely appreciate the master's benevolence in instructing me. As my joy increases, my feeling of indebtedness grows deeper."

I love this sentiment of letting go and giving up to Amida's compassion. As a foolish being, I must strive to do what is right. I must try to realize the impermanence of life. I should look to the world as a field to play out my life in gratitude. Ahh…but the smell and taste of that wonderful burrito. Knowing that I have only one day or 100 years doesn't really seem to change the life of a foolish being like me. What is of utmost importance for a foolish person such as myself is to realize that all I can really depend upon is Namo Amida Butsu and do my best to change. What about you?

Hello, Handsome

◆◆◆

When I consider deeply the vow of Amida, which arose from five kalpas of profound thought, I realize that it was for the sake of myself alone! Then how I am filled with gratitude for the Primal Vow, in which Amida resolved to save me, though I am burdened with such heavy karma.

Tannisho: Epilogue

Recently I attended the first year memorial service for Rev. Russell Hamada. It was a time of reflection on what I had lost and gained from my friendship of over twenty years with Rev. Hamada. Twenty years to some people may not seem like that long a time. However, twenty years in my life is basically my entire adult life. As I had expressed in my article about Rev. Hamada after his death, he was always there for me, through the good times and many of the very difficult ones. He was a friend that I had always felt I could turn to with any questions I may have had. We talked of our work, personal life, goals, hopes and dreams. As many of you may know, he was the person who encouraged me to enter the Institute of Buddhist Studies and eventually go on to Japan and become a *Kaikyoshi*.

There is a term in Japanese Buddhism called *zenchishiki*, meaning "good friend or teacher who leads you to the Buddhist way." Rev. Hamada was without a doubt both good friend and teacher who led me to the way. He has helped me so much in the past and continues at this moment to teach me the depth of Amida Buddha's compassion. That is a true friend.

The reason I titled this article "Hello, Handsome" is because that was the way Rev. Hamada would always greet me on the phone or often in person. No one—not even my wife—has ever referred to me as handsome. I would be shocked and would wonder what they wanted if people did refer to me as handsome. However, when Rev. Hamada said this, it seemed very natural. It was a part of his personality. He would call or I would call him on the phone and he would say, "Hello, handsome. How's it going?"

I always thought this was his way of showing his friendship and affection. This greeting was just for me. It's funny how over the years I just came to expect this greeting from him. I realized how much I had internalized the greeting when one day I heard him on the telephone, and he said, "Hello, handsome." I looked over to see if he was talking to me. To my shock, he was talking to someone else and calling him or her "handsome." As ridiculous as it may sound, I felt a little pang of jealousy when he used this phrase with someone other than me.

Rev. Hamada had a gift of relating to all people. He was one of the few people that I have ever met who could yell and argue with someone and within the hour, he would have his arm around the person and they would be talking like good friends. He would even make people whom I know he did not really like feel like a friend. He approached all people as individuals, making them feel as though his attention was just on them. Friends and enemies alike would be treated with respect.

As I have talked with others about their feelings of loss and loneliness over Rev. Hamada's death, one feels a very personal loss. I mean that although we speak of the great loss to the future of Jodo Shinshu in America and the great things Rev. Hamada could have done, we do not talk of those things so much. We speak of how much we miss him personally: his phone calls, his laugh and his zest for life. Our memories are filled with very personal recollections of conversations and meals shared. From family, friends and temple members, Russell spoke to each of us on a very personal level.

I now realize this personalized feeling is the way Amida Buddha looks at each of us. It is also the way we should each ideally interact with Amida Buddha. The quotation I began this essay with is a famous quotation of Shinran's from the *Tannisho*. Shinran, contemplating on the compassion of Amida Buddha, feels that all of Amida's practice and the reason for Amida Buddha's existence was to look out for him, Shinran alone. Shinran knows that Amida Buddha's compassion extends to all things. Yet, in his personal interaction with Amida, it is as though Amida Buddha is looking out for him. The Namo Amida Butsu that is called out by Amida is Amida Buddha calling to Shinran.

Rev. Hamada may have used the greeting "Hello, handsome" for others. However, no matter when or where I hear this phrase, it is as though he is speaking to me. As a result, I can better understand Amida Buddha's compassion for me. It is just another teaching that continues to show that my friend Russell Hamada's life did not end with his physical death. He remains a part of who and what I am. I can find and am developing this new relationship with him within the Nembutsu. As I sit in my office, I miss the phone calls or the opportunity of calling him. However, when I say "Namo Amida Butsu," it is as though Amida Buddha and Russell Hamada are responding with "Hello, handsome!" Namo Amida Butsu.

On the Back of Dragonflies

◆◆◆

Tonbo ni noote haru baru to
Ojodo kara no okyaku sama
ichinen buri no okyaku sama.
(Riding on dragonflies. Our once a year
guests are coming from the Pure Land.)
Tonbo yo tonbo aka tonbo
Mukaebi taite machimashoo
Chochin tomoshite mukae massho...
(Dragonfly, dragonfly, red dragonfly,
Lighting the bonfires and paper lanterns,
Let's greet our guests....)

"Obon no Uta" ("Song of Obon")

We all have difficulties in this life. I recently read that last year in Japan there were over 33,000 suicides. In an e-mail I received, it said there were over 2,000 missing children last year. As horrendous as all this may seem, when we hear such statistics, we are able to distance them from ourselves. Suicides and the inexplicable loss of children are usually something that happens to other people. This is the nature of most of our human compassion. It is too difficult and incomprehensible to face these horrendous facts. It is much easier to place them as events that happen somewhere else.

Although death and loss are happening on a daily basis all around us, when we personally experience the death of a loved one, our world is transformed. It is one of the most difficult of life's difficulties. In Buddhism it is called *aibetsu riku* (separation from loved ones).

Because we are so interconnected, when we lose a loved one, it feels as though a part of us has died with the person. It is more painful than I can describe in writing. It is something that can only be experienced. Those who do not know what I am talking about are either ignorant or the luckiest people on earth. Logically, if a piece of me dies when my loved one dies, then a piece of that loved one remains alive, as I live. Obon is a time to recognize the continuing relationship we have with the dead.

I don't like the idea of bringing closure to unpleasant aspects of our lives. It stinks of pop pseudo-psychology. I also don't believe Buddhism and psychology or psychotherapy are the same. The difference is that Buddhism embraces those who don't fit into the norm just as much as we embrace those who do, whereas psychology and psychotherapy try to place us in the norm.

Sorry for the side note. There is an important function to psychology and therapy. It's just not the same as Buddhism. Anyway, I don't want to close off the past. I don't want to put an end to the experience of the death of my friends and loved ones. I want to feel them in my life. Please don't suggest I need closure. I don't want to forget them, and I don't think I will ever get over the pain of losing them. However, as I live with that knowledge, through time I will learn from the pain, and if I remain open, my awareness will allow me to see how they remain a part of my life. This is Obon!

I dance with the dead. They are not ephemeral spirits and globs of ectoplasm swirling about as I dance. The song I began this article with is often sung at many temples during Obon. It is a dreadful song and only adds fuel to excluding most songs from our Buddhist services. It offends my feelings in regard to my relationship with my deceased loved ones. My friends and family are not coming back to visit me just once a year on Obon. To top it off, they are NOT riding on the back of dragonflies, particularly red dragonflies! HOW STUPID DO YOU THINK WE ARE?

No matter how quaint the imagery, it is a stupid and dangerous notion. How lonely: once a year! *My* dead family and friends are with me every day. The Pure Land touches my life each and every day. I interact with the Pure Land and my dead loved ones through Namo Amida Butsu, and they do not haunt me; they comfort me. As I interact with the world of the living, the dead interact along with me, and I interact with them on a regular basis. Obon is an opportunity for me once a year to openly acknowledge their place in my life.

Our Obon is a wonderful community event. However, it is even more important that we understand the significance of Obon. It is not about dressing up "Japanesey" or playing up to our Japanese Buddhist heritage. It is not just for the young. It is not just for women. The old should have more dead to dance with than the young. Men have just as many dead friends as women.

Do only Japanese die? No, Obon is a time for all of us to dance with the dead. What a wonderful time to celebrate their continuing existence in my life! As I dance, I can see my mom, my bachan, my dear friends—all continuing to embrace and support me within the wondrous compassion of Namo Amida Butsu. Please don't hold back. Join us, not the hundreds but the thousands of myriads of dancers, alive and dead, who make us who we are. Shall we dance?

I have to add a side note to this article I wrote long ago:
For the most part I agree with everything I have said; however, since that time I have had an experience I would like to share with you. For

many years I had ranted and raved about the song "Obon no Uta" and the imagery of my dead family and friends riding on the back of dragonflies. On one such occasion, during a memorial service for a young man named David Lew, I was explaining how ridiculous this idea was. This service was held during the middle of July. I was holding this service at the Huntsman Cancer Research Center at the University of Utah, for David had died of cancer. At this research hospital there is a beautiful restaurant and reception center with floor-to-ceiling windows overlooking Salt Lake City. This is where we were holding the service, just around dusk, and we could see the beautiful setting sun.

As I was speaking, I heard a faint tapping. It continued, and soon we were all looking toward the windows where the tapping was coming from. To my amazement and the amazement of everyone there, hundreds of golden dragonflies were hovering outside the windows. It was as if they were saying, "Not so fast." A deep feeling of joy welled up inside of me. It was as if David and the dragonflies were telling me: "You just don't know." I will leave the rest up to you, and I will continue to dance with the dead. Namo Amida Butsu.

You May Die, But Not Me

To live is to suffer; to survive is to find meaning in the suffering. If there is a purpose in life at all, there must be a purpose in suffering and dying. But no man can tell another what this purpose is. Each must find out for himself and must accept the responsibility that his answer prescribes. If he succeeds, he will continue to grow in spite of all indignities.

Gordon W. Allport, Preface to *Man's Search for Meaning*

As we express our gratitude, we must never forget that the highest appreciation is not to utter words, but to live by them.

John F. Kennedy

A few years ago, Kacie, Taylor and I were driving in the car, looking at the mountains and the changing colors around that time of year. I reminded them that the change of seasons is similar to how our lives are always changing. I asked them if they could name anything on the altar that reminded them of this change and impermanence. They both said, "The flowers!" I told them they were both right.

As usual, this little bit of competition led to an argument. I could hear them going back and forth. Kacie would say, "Dad says that life is impermanent. That means that everything dies. Everything that is alive is going to die."

Taylor responds, "No way. I'm not going to die."

"Yes, you are! I'm going to die, Dad's going to die, and Ponzu's going to die. Everything that lives will die."

"Not me," says Taylor.

"Taylor! That's why I try to be happy in the morning when I wake up. I don't know when I am going to die, so I am happy and grateful when I wake up and have another day!" says Kacie in an exasperated voice.

"Well, you can die, but I'm not going to die."

"DAAAD! Tell Taylor that she is going to die like everything else. Isn't that what you say in church!" As I get pulled into their argument, I say, "Yes, Taylor, all living things are impermanent. I don't know when, but one day we will all die."

I hear Kacie whisper to Taylor, "Seeee."

Taylor whispers back, "Well, maybe you and Dad are going to die, but I'm still not going to die!"

I still chuckle when I remember their argument. However, in reality, we all live with this argument taking place within ourselves. Rationally we can see that life is impermanent. Those of us past middle age can attest to the daily ravages of time. As we get up from the lounge chair for the commercial break, that little creak in the neck or back and slight groans that issue automatically from our mouths are witness to this inevitable change. We have had friends and close family members die much too young. Yet, how many of us with this type of personal experience still live as though we will never die?

Each night as we go to bed, can we look at the day and feel satisfied with how we left the world? Or have we gone to sleep without saying, I love you, thank you, I'm sorry, etc. to those who mean so much to us? There is a part of us that understands how we should live our lives. Yet that part is usually the quietest voice in our heads. How many times have you seen something you knew wasn't right, but didn't do or say anything? For instance, take an injustice you may have witnessed in the store or workplace. It's so easy for us to just say, "It's none of my business." There are many theories, lessons, and practices in Buddhism. However, in very simple terms, Buddhism tries to teach us how to live our lives with our thoughts, words and deeds in sync.

In Jodo Shinshu we say we live a life of gratitude. As Kacie said, when she wakes up, she tries to be happy because she knows that life is impermanent. Yet, what do you do with that gratitude or happiness? How does it affect the world? Do you believe you will live forever?

Our world, especially our current society, is falling deeper and deeper into a hell of "us" against "them." It is almost as if the worst-case scenario from my youth is playing out in our political landscape. It makes me long for the hope that was instilled in my generation with the election of John F. Kennedy, which brought me to the quote I began this month's article with. We can all express gratitude, yet how do we live by those words? I would like to close with one of my favorite quotations from the book, *The Awareness of Self*, by Rev. Gyodo Haguri:

> Generally speaking, people are considered to be good and faithful followers if they lead a moral life, attend church services and participate in welfare activities. In Jodo Shinshu Buddhism, however, while these practices are encouraged, they alone do not constitute the Buddhist way of life. What is critically important is that the teachings radically transform our way of

thinking and living so that we become true individuals: strong in crisis, humble in success, tender in our feelings and grateful at all times.

Recipe For Happiness

◆◆◆

This is the true joy in life, the being used for a purpose recognized by yourself as a mighty one; the being a force of Nature instead of a feverish, selfish little clod of ailments and grievances complaining that the world will not devote itself to making you happy. I am of the opinion that my life belongs to the whole community, and as long as I live, it is my privilege to do for it whatever I can. I want to be thoroughly used up when I die, for the harder I work the more I live. I rejoice in life for its own sake. Life is no "brief candle" to me. It is a sort of splendid torch which I have got hold of for the moment and I want to make it burn as brightly as possible before handing it on to future generations.

George Bernard Shaw, *Man and Superman: A Comedy and A Philosophy*

It is a basic human desire as expressed in our Constitution that we pursue happiness. Most of us have felt the frustration of not being able to be happy—when the happiness you had expected in life seems to be just out of your reach. At those times it is common to ask, "Why is this happening to me? What am I doing wrong? Is something wrong with me?" I don't think that happiness is eluding you or purposely avoiding you. The problem is more likely where you are looking and how you are looking for it. Although Buddhism is a path to discover who you are, the answer may not be exactly what you expect. Maybe the "you" that you are searching for isn't the "you" that you expect to find.

When Shakyamuni Buddha began his search, he had received almost every material pleasure a human being living at that time could imagine. His father had made certain that he would live a life of luxury. He had palaces for each season. He was said to have been blessed with great intelligence, physical strength, and good looks. His wife was said to have been beautiful and intelligent. He was blessed with a son. Yet happiness still eluded him. How many of you feel that if you had wealth, health and a happy family, you would have happiness? I doubt that Shakyamuni Buddha had a cell phone, cable TV, the Internet, microwave ovens or fast food. Materially, each of us reading this is probably better off than he was.

In our present age, we are constantly bombarded with media about celebrities. These are individuals who have wealth, seemingly good health, fame, and usually, physical beauty. Yet, we are always hearing about their stints in various rehabilitation facilities. Even these facilities are described as being luxurious, where all their physical needs are met. Why have they not been able to find happiness?

George Bernard Shaw wrote the quote at the beginning of this essay. Probably his best-known work is *Pygmalion*, which was made into the musical *My Fair Lady*. Shaw was a self-taught writer and devout socialist. He lived to the age of ninety-four. He died from injuries sustained in a fall from a ladder while working on his property. I was sent the above quote in an email. The quote is a compilation of various writings attributed to Shaw. I believe that the essence of this quote is in the idea that happiness in life can be found in service to the community.

In this quote he writes, "Life is no 'brief candle' to me." This particular line struck a harmonious chord within me. This past July I turned fifty. Before my birthday I had told Carmela that when I was in my twenties, I had three very good friends with whom I had discussed the subject of how long we would probably live. In our discussions we had talked about how we have had the privilege of living full and exciting lives. As a result we were probably burning through our lives at a higher rate than normal and that we would probably not live much longer than fifty. Each of these friends had encouraged me in trying to work for the sake of the community. I have written about the guidance I had received from Rev. Russell Hamada and Rev. Dennis Yoshikawa about the importance of our lives within the Sangha. While I was at the University of Utah, my friend who would become Senator Pete Suazo had encouraged me to work for the sake of equality and the community here in Utah. All three of my friends have died, each before the age of fifty.

Carmela had told me that since I didn't die before fifty, as I had somewhat expected, my premonitions of death at fifty weren't about a physical death, but a psychological death. I believe that she was right. Each of us is being born and dying daily. We place limitations upon who and what we are. We create our own realities of happiness and unhappiness; both are waiting for us. If we create a world in which our focus is "me, me, me," or as Shaw has described, "a feverish, selfish little clod of ailments and grievances complaining that the world will not devote itself to making you happy," then this happiness will always be just out of reach. Our bonno (greed, anger, ignorance) is like a hungry ghost, never satisfied.

Yet we can create a world in which we work for the betterment of all—where our happiness can be found in the happiness of others. There is a quote in my minister's *Seiten* that I often read: "Our life is filled with warmth in sharing life with others. It is a simple truth to learn, but a difficult practice to fully realize. In personal life, it means to act by placing ourselves in the position of another; in community life, it means to give service with joy and gratitude for the betterment of all. The practice of making others happy is based upon the clear understanding of life, which is oneness. In deep gratitude, let us realize this oneness of all life, the heart of which is compassion." This seems to be a recipe for happiness in this life. Namo Amida Butsu!

My Inheritance

♦♦♦

The mind-light that takes all in, keeps them
Always illuminated and well protected,
Though the darkness of ignorance is already
Broken through,
The dense clouds of greed and infatuation,
Of anger and hate,
On hovering over the sky of true faith.
It is like the sunlight veiled by the clouds,
Behind the clouds, the brightness reigns
and there is no darkness.

Shoshin Nembutsu Ge

I had tried to imagine the scenario of how I would accept the news. Or I had hoped that I would be with her. I had expected the world to stop. Maybe it did—my world—for a while.

As I was walking outside, the sun was still shining, though the blue of the Utah sky seemed a little somber. The birds were singing in a slightly harmonic key. I had hoped to wake up in San Jose from a bad dream. Maybe I was still in the dream and hadn't heard the alarm. I was probably late for the Lotus Preschool morning service. Yet no matter how I hoped for this dream to end, here I was in Salt Lake City. The woman who had given me life and shown me unconditional love had died the night before, as I was riding on a plane to be with her.

How can I tell my mother I love her? What can I say to comfort my father and family? Why am I still alive? I'm a priest. "Say something then. Be strong. You've studied all kinds of books. You've spoken words of consolation to other people who have lost their mothers. Listen to the Dharma. Say the Nembutsu. Namo Amida Butsu. Open Sesame! Mom's still dead!" All of these thoughts ran through my mind and some of them still continue.

Here I was, faced with one of the major sufferings that I had studied. *Aibetsuriku* (separation from those one loves) is one of the most painful of the eight sufferings. Yet this is something that all of us must go through at one time or another. We cannot bring back the dead, yet we can understand and find meaning in that death for ourselves. This is what Buddhism offers.

I had read and heard other ministers speak of the story of Kisagotami. Kisagotami was a woman who had lost her only child. Because of the depth of her grief, she wandered the streets asking people to bring back her child. The people of her village just figured she was crazy. Yet was she so crazy? Isn't this feeling of wanting our loved ones back something all of us feel? If Kisagotami was crazy, so am I.

One day the Buddha came to Kisagotami's small village. She had heard that the Buddha was a wondrous person who could help with anything. So she immediately sought out the Buddha to help her with the unbearable loneliness that she felt.

Once she found the Buddha, she pleaded, "Please help my baby. Please bring my baby back to me!"

The Buddha calmly replied, "I will help you. Yet you must do something to help. Find three mustard seeds from one of the families in this village who have never experienced the death of a loved one, and then I can help you." Kisagotami was overjoyed to hear that the Buddha could help her.

She quickly set out door-to-door trying to find a family who had not experienced the death of a loved one. As she searched the village, she could not find a single family that had not experienced such a thing. As she was going from door to door, she slowly realized what the Buddha's purpose was in sending her out for the seeds. All of us must lose someone we love. This is a part of life. Understanding this, Kisagotami returned to the Buddha and gave the lifeless child to the Buddha and asked him to hold a funeral for her baby. From that time, she became a devout follower of the Buddha's teaching.

I'm sure many of you have heard this story. If you were like me, you may have passed it off as a nice story for Dharma school students. Yet this story is relevant for each of us who must some day be separated from those we love. I, like Kisagotami giving up her baby to Buddha, must also give up my mother to Buddha, Amida Buddha. In giving up my mother, I know she is fine. It is for myself that I must try to understand the Nembutsu. I must find the meaning and significance of my mother's death—not for her, but for myself. It is because of her that I know the Buddha's teachings. I am not alone in my grief, and the Buddha's teachings are with me.

Hopefully, each of you will take the time to understand the teachings before you are in a situation of personal tragedy. But it will not be easy. Jodo Shinshu is considered to be the easiest yet most difficult religion. We always hear phrases such as, "Amida will save all beings. Just say the Nembutsu." This phrase is nothing but words upon a page. Shinran Shonin says in the *Tannisho*, Chapter Two:

> If the original vow of Amida is true,
> Then Shakyamuni's sermons cannot be untrue.
> If the Buddha's words are true,
> Zendo's commentaries cannot be untrue.
> How can Honen's sayings be false?
> If Honen's sayings are true,
> What I, Shinran, say cannot possibly be false, either.
> After all is said, such is the faith of this simpleton.
> Beyond this, it is entirely left up to each one of you
> Whether you accept and believe in the Nembutsu or reject it.

We must each find a meaning for the Nembutsu teachings in our own lives, for it can help. It has helped me. My mother has helped me in my life and in her death. On this overcast Tuesday, as I walk out of my house to cross the street to the temple, the light is shining and the sky is bright. As the lines from the *Shoshinge* that I began this article with state:

> The dense clouds of greed and infatuation, of anger and hate,
> On hovering over the sky of true faith.
> It is like the sunlight veiled by the clouds;
> Behind the clouds, the brightness reigns and there is no darkness.

The sky in Salt Lake or San Jose may be cloudy or sunny and blue. Yet with the Nembutsu teaching, "Namo Amida Butsu," which my mother helped me to understand, "brightness reigns and there is no darkness." When I feel lonely, I know that my mother is with Amida, and when I say "Namo Amida Butsu," I, too, am with Amida and with my mother again. They are always with me. Thanks, Mom. You have left me the greatest inheritance I could ever hope or ask for. Namo Amida Butsu.

When the Winds of Impermanence Blow

◆ ◆ ◆

The fragile nature of human life underlies both the young and the old. We should therefore, all the sooner, turn our hearts to the singularly important matter of True Life. We should recite the Nembutsu upon having completely entrusted all that we are to the Buddha Amida. Listen to these words. Please listen to these words.

Rennyo Shonin, "Letter on White Ashes"

I knew that things weren't going well when all the people seemed to appear out of nowhere. I thought I was on the ground when I realized I was lying in the hospital bed. Doctors and nurses were stripping off all my clothes and poking me all over with needles. When I tried to look around, there was a bright light shining down and all sorts of worried faces staring at me. My feet and hands were freezing, and the cold was slowly moving up my body. The one source of warmth was from the nurse, holding my hand and encouraging me: "Stay with us,

Jerry. Stay with us."

One doctor seemed to be frantically trying to push a needle into the area between my shoulder and chest. It hurt like hell and it was making me mad that he couldn't seem to find a vein. I also kept thinking, "I'm all right; I'm all right" when I heard one of the nurses say, "His pulse is very low and his blood pressure is dropping."

I don't know why they did it, but at about the same time the nurse said this, the doctor stopped pushing the needle around and they covered my face with the bed sheet. Suddenly, I thought, "Maybe I'm not all right. But don't give up, folks. I'm still here. Thank you for all your hard work." With that realization, I quit fighting things and felt a deep appreciation for the people around me. I thought of my girls and Carmela and hoped that if I died, they would be okay.

But I didn't want to die. I tried to calm down and accept things as they were. I took deep breaths and began to slowly recite "Na Man Da Bu… Na Man Da Bu…." The anger began to fade and a feeling of deep gratitude for all these strangers working for my benefit filled me. I thought how easy it would be to just let go. But I could feel the warmth in the nurse's hand. It felt like life encouraging me on.

The next thing I remember was that I was in some sort of operating room talking to a male nurse named Eddis who was Mormon and used to live in Utah. In my groggy state of mind, I remember their telling me a doctor was going to try to find why I was bleeding. I don't remember much, but the next memory was of being in the Critical Care Unit of the hospital. The nurse in there looked exactly like Sarah Palin. She was extremely kind, but stern. I asked if I could get up to go to the bathroom or if she would at least get me a bedpan. She said to just go in the bed; I wasn't to move.

I couldn't hold it and just let go, but it turned out it was just a lot of blood. I felt cold again and she called the doctor. I heard them say my color had changed to almost white. They once again began attaching tubes with different types of liquid and blood.

The next step was hearing another doctor introduce himself and explain that he wanted to take out my entire colon. He said, "If you don't stop bleeding, you will die. If I take out a part of your colon and it isn't the site of the bleeding, I have to go back in and take out the entire colon. I recommend the removal of all of it at once." I asked him to call Carmela, since they had already told me she was on the way to the hospital. After I heard him talking to Carmela, I just felt as though I wanted to sleep. I could trust Carmela with my life. All of this had happened within twenty-four hours.

I am happy to report that I am doing well and resting at home, although I did end up spending four days in the ICU and a couple of days in the recovery area of the hospital. Carmela told me I must have died in the hospital since I didn't have a blood pressure. It was quite an experience. It's amazing how so many things can happen so quickly. As the "Letter on White Ashes" says, "The fragile nature of human life underlies both the young and old."

I had been at the BCA Ministers' Summer Fuken (study seminar and meeting) in Reno, Nevada. I had just completed chairing the meeting. I felt very relieved and relaxed. My stomach was feeling a little uneasy, and when I went to the toilet, I saw fresh blood. I tried to ignore it, but it scared me a little.

I tried to call Carmela, but she was in a meeting in Salt Lake. I went to dinner with some of my friends and just didn't feel right. When we were leaving the restaurant, I was feeling a little weak, and I could barely keep my eyes open since the sun felt so bright. It was as though my eyes had been dilated. The blue sky looked white. I asked Rev. Matsumoto to take me back to the hotel and said that I wouldn't be able to attend evening service.

When I got back to the room, I called Carmela, explaining my physical discomfort. She immediately told me to call 911 and go directly to the emergency room at the nearest hospital. I told her absolutely not. I said I was going to go to sleep and that things would be better in the morning. I think this was my first stupid mistake. I didn't want to feel embarrassed about going to the hospital. My ego was telling me that it wasn't dignified. She had me set up the Skype video phone service on my laptop so she could monitor me throughout the night. I agreed to that, but felt silly.

The next morning she told me she had called my primary care

physician and he had told her to tell me to go directly to the hospital. Once again, I didn't want to call for an ambulance. How embarrassing! I told her I was going to pack up, check out and have Rev. Matsumoto take me to the ER. By the time I got to the front desk, I felt a little disoriented and tired. I must have looked pale, because Rev. Matsumoto looked worried and took my suitcase and Rev. Harada checked me out of the hotel. Some of the other ministers were checking out and wondering what was going on. I said I just felt a little weak, so I was leaving early.

Once I arrived at the hospital, they immediately admitted me and set me up for a colonoscopy and observation. I told Rev. Matsumoto to go home and that I would be fine. He must have been in the waiting room for five hours as they waited for a room to open up. He told me Rev. Harada had changed his flight and was staying in Reno with me.

Instead of being grateful, I felt embarrassed at all the trouble I was causing my friends. It turns out my friends would be saving my life. Right before the ordeal I mentioned at the beginning of this essay, I asked Rev. Harada to call the nurse, for I needed to go to the bathroom. He called her, and as I was trying to go to the bathroom, that is when I collapsed and ended up losing about half of my blood volume. The healing physically and mentally began when I began to accept rather than resist this flurry of bodhisattvas who surrounded me.

In the "Letter on White Ashes," Rennyo encourages us to focus on True Life. I believe that True Life is realizing that we cannot live on our own. We live as the result of countless causes and conditions beyond our personal ability. We live because of the good intentions of others. It is due to this deep compassion that surrounds us in spite of ourselves that we survive. I was lucky enough to see it very clearly manifested by this important life experience.

I hope that my ego has diminished a little and my mind has opened to allow me to be a little more open to the compassion that surrounds me. Yes, even someone like Sarah Palin holds a place in my life. I realized that she is more than just the character I have seen portrayed in the media. I can no longer judge a book by its cover. Death is easy. It really doesn't scare me. Yet I will hold on to this precious life for as long as I can—until the winds of impermanence once again blow and my eyes are closed forever.

This life that I think is mine is a gift given to me by countless bodhisattvas sending forth oceans of wisdom, compassion and love. I hope to and will strive to live my life worthy of this net of compassion that embraces me by living a life of gratitude. Thank you, everyone, for your well wishes. Namo Amida Butsu.

The Realm of Gratitude

◆ ◆ ◆

Many things occur in our human lives. But, whatever difficulties or sadness that we may have experienced, if we can look upon our lives as being rare and wondrous events, then we truly will have lived. If we are able to realize this realm of gratitude, in which we are able to live—and die—in gassho, then what else could we need?

Jitsuen Kakehashi, *Bearer of the Light: The Life and Thought of Rennyo*

This is the time of year when I really appreciate the idea of transformation and impermanence in my life. It is one of the fundamental teachings in Buddhism. All around me the Earth calls us to wake up and see true and real life. The spring flowers burst forth out of the fallen leaves of autumn. Life is born out of the debris and silent death that winter brings. The green grasses of spring seem to sing and stretch forth from the yellow sod. The Earth understands that in life there is death and life again.

However, we live in a world where permanence is stressed. We try to hold on to our youth, forgetting the knowledge that our age has given us. In our lives we are stressed out by the natural changes to our physical conditions. Shakyamuni Buddha proclaimed that birth, sickness, old age and death were the natural conditions of our lives. If we only focus on and hold on to these four sufferings as problems rather than as natural occurrences, we may actually be wasting that which we are so fearful of losing: life itself!

Even after years of studying Buddhism and knowing of these truths, I put myself beyond this truth. As I watch the blooming of spring, I seem to not want to acknowledge the browning and hardening of my own core. I must force myself to look at the change in my life. Where once there may have been a spring, I am now facing the autumn. In embracing this truth, I must acknowledge the changing world around me.

Critics of Buddhism often point to the first Noble Truth, "Life is suffering," as proof that our teachings are negative and pessimistic. This is an extremely shallow understanding of this truth. While this first truth points out the fact that in life there is suffering, the other three truths point out a way to alleviate these sufferings. In addition, the idea that life is suffering stems from a deeper existential dilemma: that for me to live, something else must die.

All of us would like to live a life without sickness. I believe this is an unattainable wish, and there is so much we learn from our illnesses. As for old age, I find that as I grow older, I appreciate the fullness of what I am given, from the laughter of my children to the sound of my bones creaking in the morning as I awake. I am still alive! This realm of gratitude is the life of Nembutsu. It is in the impermanence of each moment in life—moving forward—that I am allowed to appreciate this life I have been given. Shakyamuni Buddha said, "Do not vainly lament, but wonder at the law of transiency.... Do not cherish the unworthy desire that the changeable might become unchanging."

As a result of this dynamic life force, which we Jodo Shinshu Buddhists refer to as Amida Buddha's call, I am allowed to appreciate my life. In Japanese there is a word *shoji*. It consists of the characters for life and death. It expresses the knowledge that both are one. As something lives, it dies at the same time, moment after moment. Our life is shoji.

I remember playing bubbles with my children. We laughed and enjoyed the beauty of the bubbles. They glowed in the light as they flittered along the wind. The beauty of bubbles is in their fragile nature—their glow as they are embraced in the light and the sound of my children at play. Isn't the beauty of our lives and this life force the knowledge that we are all impermanent? To live forever would only mute the beauty and sound. Our lives are transformed moment after moment, living and dying, always embraced in the compassion of Amida Buddha. Let us try not to hold on to that which cannot be held on to. Life and death are one. As the Earth itself teaches us this lesson of birth and death, living and dying, let us live in the realm of gratitude, appreciating both are essential aspects of who and what we are. This is the life of Nembutsu. This is the sound of Namo Amida Butsu.